LIFE-25

LIFE-25

*Interviews with Prisoners
Serving Life Sentences*

P. J. Murphy and

Loyd Johnsen

NEW STAR BOOKS
VANCOUVER
1997

Published by New Star Books Ltd., 2504 York Avenue, Vancouver, BC
V6K 1E3. All rights reserved. No part of this work may be reproduced or
used in any form or by any means – graphic, electronic, or mechanical –
without the prior written permission of the publisher. Any request for pho-
tocopying or other reprographic copying must be sent in writing to the
Canadian Copyright Licensing Agency (CANCOPY), 6 Adelaide Street
East, Suite 900, Toronto, ON M5C 1H6.

Editing and production by Carolyn Stewart and Rolf Maurer
Cover design by James Lewis
Cover photo by Ted Dave
Printed and bound in Canada
1 2 3 4 5   01 00 99 98 97

Publication of this book is made possible by grants from the Canada Council and the Cultural Services Branch, Province of British Columbia.

Canadian Cataloguing in Publication Data

Johnsen, Loyd, 1943-
Life-25

Includes bibliographical references.
ISBN 0-921586-55-8
1. Life imprisonment – Canada. 2. Prisoners – Canada – Interviews.
3. Prison sentences – Canada. I. Murphy, Peter, 1946- II. Title.
HV9308.J63 1996   365'.4'092   C96-910677-7

CONTENTS

For Tony Parker, master of the tape recorder,
whose books on prison beckoned us on.

'He who speaks, he who writes is above all one who speaks
on behalf of all those who have no voice.'
— VICTOR SERGE

ACKNOWLEDGMENTS

A project such as this would not have been possible without the assistance of many helping hands over the years. Research grants from the Canada Council (Explorations Grant) and the Social Sciences and Humanities Research Council of Canada enabled us to undertake the project in the first place.

Many officials of the Correctional Service of Canada (CSC) facilitated our research, which had received the personal endorsement of the commissioner of the CSC at that time (1990), Mr. Ole Ingstrup. Of special note are Harold Golden of Regional Headquarters (Pacific), who arranged clearances and passes for the follow-up interviews which we carried out in 1994-95, and Dave McLaren, director of the Staff Training College in Mission, who allowed us to spend several days searching through the thirty-odd boxes of the CSC Library that had been transferred to his offices in the summer of 1995.

The first transcriptions of our interviews were ably carried out by Joanna Dudley and Marlene Johnsen; further editings and revisions were assisted by Debbie Simoneau and Joanne Doidge of the Arts and Education Faculty at the University College of the Cariboo; Jennifer Murphy did final editing and proofreading.

Finally, and foremost, we would like to thank those men who agreed to be interviewed and whose stories and thoughts make up this book. It is their book as much as ours and we appreciated their frank answers to our battery of questions, especially since it was clear from the very beginning that they could in no way profit from this project – except insofar as their reflections might throw some light on the complex and controversial issue of the life-25 sentence and the attendant issue in recent years of the fifteen-year judicial review.

PREFACE

Loyd Johnsen and I began working on *Life-25* in 1989-90, when we were both teaching in the Simon Fraser University Prison Education Program at Kent Maximum Security in Agassiz, BC. For five years I had coordinated the program and taught English, while Loyd coordinated the General Educational Development (GED) and upgrading programs. Over this period of time we met many men, some of them our students, who had been convicted of first-degree murder and were sentenced to life-25 – life imprisonment without eligibility for parole for twenty-five years.

The twenty-five-year minimum sentences were the result of a series of compromises effected in 1976 when capital punishment was abolished in Canada. On the one hand, they marked a movement towards a more humane and civil society; but on the other, they marked a dramatic increase in the length of sentences being handed out. Under Section 745 of the Criminal Code, these new lifers were not eligible for parole until they had served twenty-five years of their sentence, *unless* they were successful in their fifteen-year judicial review. The judicial review was only an opportunity for the prisoner to appeal his eligibility date for a parole hearing and nothing to do with the parole process itself

Prior to 1976, many of the men we interviewed would not have received a first-degree sentence; instead, they would have received a second-degree sentence and, as the statistics for that period show, would have served on average ten years before parole eligibility. In other words, some of the lifers we interviewed would not even have been in prison at the time we talked to them if they had been sentenced before the passing of Bill C-84 in 1976. One of the great ironies in the public outcry over the fifteen-year judicial review is that it is rarely pointed out that, far from "cheating" the system of time owed, the life-25 men serve more time than had been formerly demanded.

These extremely long sentences are very difficult to comprehend or to imagine, quite literally so since no one has yet served one to term. This book affords the men who were sentenced to life-25 an opportunity to voice their views on the subject. These voices, seldom heard in the various debates that have grown up around this new type of sentencing, are essential to a balanced appraisal of the life-25 sentence and the fifteen-year judicial review.

Our position as outsiders who worked on the inside and who were not directly affiliated with the Correctional Service of Canada (CSC) helped us gain the confidence of the men we interviewed. We were not academic researchers in the area (criminologists or social scientists of various persuasions) and we were obviously not researchers working for the CSC (whom those serving time view with much apprehension). Besides, we weren't engaged in collecting data; we were interested in conducting a series of interviews that would constitute an oral history of how men serving life-25 see their situations. While the CSC officially sanctioned our project, it did not supply financial support of any sort and did not have access to, or control over, our findings. Commissioner Ole Ingstrup's support for our project coincided with his own Task Force on Long-Term Sentences (1991).

There was a flurry of interest in the life-25 sentences when they were first introduced, but within ten years this new group of lifers had become one of the most neglected in the prison population.

This situation changed dramatically at the appearance of the first candidates for the fifteen-year judicial review: if their review was successful, they could then appeal to the parole board for a reduction in their eligibility dates. Out of sight, out of mind was certainly no longer the case with those doing life-25. The public outcry and political protest over Section 745 of the Criminal Code, which dealt with judicial review, were mounting steadily at the time we began conducting the interviews. It was as if a time bomb was set off in the media each time there was a new applicant for judicial review.

Over a two-year period (1989-90) we tape-recorded twenty interviews with first-degree murderers who were serving their sentences in the various institutions that make up the Pacific Region of the CSC (Kent, Matsqui, Mountain, William Head, Ferndale, and Elbow Lake). Fifteen of these interviews were chosen for inclusion in *Life-25*. We also interviewed fifteen men who were serving life sentences for second-degree murder (also sentenced to life but eligible for parole after ten to twenty years). This second set of interviews, none of which were used in the present collection, served an important function, however, in clarifying for us the unique features of the life-25 sentence. Men sentenced to second-degree murder were, of course, facing "big time" and, even though they obviously shared some similar views on what it meant to work through such long sentences, they did, generally speaking, have a very different attitude towards their sentence in that it seemed to lie within their grasp in so far as parole eligibility dates and such could be calculated and worked toward. This second set of interviews also made it painfully obvious that the distinction between a first and second-degree conviction is, in many cases, very difficult to discern and that often the deciding factors owe little to clearly defined processes of judicial reasoning.

The control group also enabled us to see from the beginning that our focus needed to be on the nature of the life-25 sentence itself. We set up a two-part interview format (each of which lasted an hour to an hour and a half). The first part dealt, in a flexible manner, with "Today and Yesterday" and raised questions concerning the present situation of the interviewee, family background, schooling, work history and personal relationships. The second interview dealt with "Today and Tomorrow." Here we raised questions that were central to our interests: how a life-25 inmate expected or imagined his sentence to progress in terms of reviews, required programs, transfers to lower security and, finally, parole; how he compared himself to others serving shorter sentences and how he got along with these other groups; how he had adjusted or changed psychologically in trying to come to terms with the life-25 sentence and what further changes could be anticipated; how did he think the whole question of life-25 sentences might be reviewed or reconceived; and – finally – how he saw himself on release, who would he be then?

We were not interested in "true crime" sensationalism and let each man decide how little or how much to say on the subject of the murder that led to his conviction. For many it was obviously a painful experience to relive the events through a re-telling. The outspoken nature of many of the interviews on these and other topics was encouraged by a number of guarantees we made concerning confidentiality. No one but ourselves would be privy to the taped interviews and when we were finished with them they would be physically destroyed. Pseudonyms would be used and all actual place names or names of other people would be altered. If any reference in an interview threatened anonymity, it was deleted. The men we talked to stood to gain nothing personally by doing so; therefore, we ensured that they also did not put themselves at risk of losing anything by statements that could be construed as detrimental to their position in prison or in subsequent reviews and parole hearings.

The fundamental question of time passing, of a sentence being formulated, was built into the very structure of *Life-25* in two ways.

First of all, the fifteen interviews were arranged in the only way that made sense given our focus on the nature of the life-25 sentence: in chronological order, progressing from those who had the least time in through to those who had done progressively more time (the last entry was, in fact, sentenced pre-1976). Secondly, after we had completed the transcription, editing, and arrangement of the fifteen interviews in 1992-93, we decided to wait another two years in order to carry out a series of updates for each interviewee that would supplement the longitudinal dimensions of our cross-sectional sampling.

There is a chorus of voices calling for the full force of the life-25 sentence to be brought to bear on those convicted of first-degree murder: politicians, victims' rights groups, grass-roots political initiatives – all have received favourable media coverage of their views and positions. The issues are complex ones which are often grossly oversimplified by calls for political reforms that are merely expedient or opportunistic rather than thoughtful deliberations. The voices of those most qualified to speak about these life-25 sentences are the very ones most often excluded from the discussion; namely, the men who are serving them. And our aim throughout the time we worked on this project was simply to supply a means by which these men could give voice to their thoughts and feelings about the life-25 sentence.

P. J. Murphy
Kamloops, BC
January 1997

GLOSSARY

Pacific Region prisons (by security level):

Kent (maximum)
general population and protective custody population

Matsqui (medium [high])
general population only

Mission (medium)
general population and protective custody population

Mountain (medium)
protective custody population only

William Head (medium [low])
general population and protective custody population

Elbow Lake (minimum)
general population and protective custody population

Ferndale (minimum)
general population and protective custody population

Regional Psychiatric Centre (RPC) (now the Regional Health Centre)
for treatment of personality disorders and addictions

Special Handling Unit (SHU) (maximum [high])
for inmates who seriously assault or kill staff or other inmates. (There is no SHU in the Pacific Region.)

Oakalla
a former multi-level provincial facility; besides housing provincial inmates (sen-

*tences of less than two years), Oakalla
also housed those on trial for a capital
crime and, before the end of capital punishment, it was home to Death Row*

Sentences for murder (general definitions that hold true for cases in this book):

First-degree   *premeditated or in the commission of a crime against a person; carries an automatic life-25 sentence (i.e. a life sentence with parole eligibility after twenty-five years)*

Second-degree   *intentional but not premeditated; carries a life sentence with a parole eligibility date of ten to twenty years*

Manslaughter   *neither premeditated nor intentional; usually carries a sentence of less than fifteen years with no life term attached*

Note 1: Life term: regardless of the offender's status (in prison or on parole) the Crown has absolute control over his or her freedom. There is no expiry to the offender's parole. Even a suspicion by a parole officer that the offender might reoffend is enough to have him or her re-arrested.

Note 2: Judicial Review: as noted in the introduction, a judicial review is an opportunity offered those serving life-25 to plead their case for an early parole eligibility. It has nothing to do with the parole process itself; it only allows the inmate to apply for parole. At the time of the interview only one of those included in the book has had a successful review. William had his parole eligibility reduced from twenty-five years to twenty-two years.

Expressions used in this book:

AA   *Alcoholics Anonymous, a support group for recovering alcoholics*

B&E   *breaking and entering*

beef   *type of crime (e.g. murder beef, sex beef)*

bit	*sentence (e.g. ten-year bit)*
book	*life sentence (e.g. "doing book")*
bugs	*inmates others see as annoying or crazy*
bug juice	*any drug used to calm an inmate*
CSC	*Correctional Service of Canada*
date	*sentence expiry date (lifers have no "date")*
double-bunking	*two people to a cell*
fish	*new inmate*
general population (GP)	*all inmates except those requiring special protection*
hole	*segregation unit (usually 23-hour lockup)*
house	*prison cell*
Hut	*short for Quonset Hut, a housing unit in Mountain Institution*
ITF	*internal transfer of funds used by inmates to purchase goods*
job	*anything an inmate does in prison to legally earn money (e.g. library clerk, student, etc.); the top wage at the time of the interviews was $5.25 per day*
K-Unit	*a protective custody unit in Kent Institution*
mission statement	*In 1989, CSC issued a 'mission statement' which stated, among other things, that 'all offenders must have opportunities to serve their sentences in a meaningful and dignified manner and our programs must provide for personal growth within the institutional setting.' The mission statement was met with great cynicism by both staff and prisoners*

movement	*scheduled movements of inmates at Kent and Matsqui*
mandatory supervision	*usually when two thirds of an inmate's sentence is complete, he or she is released to a halfway house*
PFV	*private family visit; every prison has a small cabin for an inmate and his family to use for a two-day visit*
piped	*hit on the head with a metal pipe*
PN	*performance notice; until recently, if an inmate broke a rule, an Unsatisfactory Performance Notice (UPN) was handed out; if an inmate did an exemplary job, an Excellent Performance Notice (EPN) was warranted*
protective custody (PC)	*at Kent Institution, inmates who require protection from the general population comprise protective custody (e.g. sexual offenders, "rats" or cell thieves, and those heavily indebted to other inmates)*
range	*a tier of six to eight cells*
rats	*informers*
seg	*segregation unit (the hole)*
sentence expiry	*the end of a full sentence*
SFU	*Simon Fraser University, which until 1992 offered a prison education program at a number of prisons in the Fraser Valley*
shank	*a large homemade knife*
short	*an inmate who is within months of being released*
skinner	*an inmate convicted of a sexual assault*
unit	*a cell block (usually four ranges - two upper, two lower)*

MARK

'I know for a fact, I mean, I'm not a violent person.'

Mark was twenty-three years old when sentenced to life-25. He had served two years at the time of his interview.

My mother, my foster mother, well, hated me. I was mischievous. She went a little psychotic on me. My father was always fair, eh. You know the punishment would always fit the crime. At least he was there more or less to teach me the right, not the wrong, rather than punish, rather than my mother's pretty weird stuff. She tried to starve me. Couldn't eat at the table, and when I did eat, I'd eat off the porch, and if that wasn't enough food to sustain myself, I'd steal it from the house.

My real parents? Well, I remember back when I was about four years old, I was with my real parents. They were both alcoholics who lived in Quesnel near the river, the Fraser River. And there was a small stream going out into the river. My dad used to bring up fish from the river now and again. Basically it was low living conditions. And then I was told my father had died, fallen down the stairs and broke his neck. I wound up being sent to, what I was told to be, my grandmother's. It was on a large farm and there was a couple of other kids there. It was lots of good eating. And it was a pretty happy atmosphere. And then, when I was about five, I was put on a Greyhound bus, and I lived with what I knew as my aunt and uncle and my cousin, a teenage girl.

And then my mother came one day, just out of the blue, and I was so happy, right? I had been dreaming about my mother for so long. I wanted to see her, and then there she was, walking up the path. And she came to take me away to Kamloops. She had remarried; I didn't know who the heck he was. We were staying in a small motel in some downtown area. And I was basically left free. Whether or not she was neglecting me or whether it was her philosophy to let a child do whatever he pleases, I'm not really sure, but I was happy. I mean I never had any really stringent rules, right? The only thing is, you know, come home for beddies. There was no scrutiny of any of my actions. So I could just come home, open the refrigerator, eat what I wanted, drink what I wanted, and basically head 'er back on my way, or whatever, eh. And perhaps that's some of the problems that led up to when I was adopted.

The first foster home that I was actually aware of was when I was six years old. I was there for a year I think. Perhaps a little less. At the second one, I stayed there for about a year, too. Then I was moved to another foster home. And that one was in the same city, but I have no idea where. And I stayed there for about a year. And then when I was nine I was adopted.

Each time, everything would be a complete change. The only actual constant in any of the situations was some of my personal belongings. If you can imagine changing families just once in your life. The amount of things that you learned, that are no longer relevant in your present situation, is huge.

When I was five years old at my mother's, it was basically, no such thing as meal time. It was eat when you're hungry. Which to me is logical, natural and entirely reasonable. I mean why eat when you're not hungry? Why not eat when you are hungry? Then there was: Okay, we're going to divide food three times. You're allowed food here, here and here. The other times you can do anything but food. So that was something to deal with.

Then when you go deeper than that, table manners. With my mom there was basically no need for table manners, I mean within reason. You couldn't shove things in your mouth and talk with your mouth open with the food falling out. But with these other families, they went past the point of bad manners to: The fork is held in your left hand and the knife in your right. You place the fork here, you place the knife here. The glass is always here. Never turn your plate when you're eating. And then when you change to another family, their eating rules might be completely different. They might be the elbows on the table, and, you know, gimme that plate of beans over there. I mean, the whole atmosphere changes.

Not only that, the food does too. I mean what you're eating at one house isn't going to be what you're eating at another. And your mind, as well as your body, has to undergo this change. There's familiar places; places that you would normally go to have fun are no longer there. Other things change – like friends, right? For me, I would know somebody for approximately one year, and then they were history – completely. The house, some of the toys that you're used to playing with.

I am only a government object; I can be moved and replaced at will in any position. And I'm not to have contact at all with my previous families. Who am I that I must take a trail completely different than everybody else?

When I look back, most of the time I definitely felt lost. But I didn't know this was out of the ordinary. I mean, people had come and gone; parents had come and gone; places had come and gone. But the ways that I felt didn't usually have anything to do with the disappearing friends, the disappearing parents, the disappearing places, and the disappearing pets. I don't think that those affected me as much as having to deal with a new situation all of a sudden.

I'm sure each person likes to get into some kind of routine so that at least some things in the next day are going to be foreseeable. At least there's not going to be something so out of the ordinary happening tomorrow that nothing is the same as the day before.

There was no real concept in my mind that the next day would be the same as the day before. And, of course, I conducted my life accordingly. I went with the flow. And I didn't plan anything ahead. I still don't. If I plan something, it generally falls through. I have no practice at it, right? So, I don't. It's like, if I open my eyes tomorrow, I'll probably live through the day.

I've always had this sort of belief that anyone who trusts me won't be let down, but those who don't trust me won't be let down either. So, basically, when I was mistrusted I would be untrustworthy, and usually that wound me up being in quite a bit of trouble, because, of course, I was considered a problem child because of some of the things that happened in the foster families.

The first foster family, the government just came in, took me away all of a sudden one day. I remember I was in the living room with my mother and this guy drove up and basically just picked me up and started walking away with me. Me and my mother were crying and he took me away. He took me to the Ballistas. He was a carpenter, not rich, but doing fairly well. He had two children, a girl and a boy. And the problems we had there weren't serious or anything. It was me and the boy didn't get along. We were about the same age but he was bigger than I was. And me and him used to battle, battle all the time, right? I mean just over anything. As far as I remember, neither one of us ever got hurt during these battles, but I guess it caused sufficient alarm for the mother and the family to eventually say that I was just a bad kid, right? I'm the outsider. But that makes sense, actually.

From there, I guess there must be some kind of record or something, right? You know, incompatible situations. And that's the one constant in all of this. Like they don't take into account the possibility that there's something wrong with these places. They automatically say that, well, you didn't work out in these places, so you are the bad apple.

Anyways this family, the Cains, came and looked me over, and I guess, you know, kicked my tires. Then the government dude showed up and he says, do you want to live with this family? I'm only seven years old at this point. I'm a little tired of getting dragged around all over the place, right? But, you know, still just a stupid kid anyway. So, he says, I'll tell you what, you spend a month with these people, and if you like them, then you can stay there.

So, they took me away, brought all my stuff along, which wasn't much, right? I had a bike. They were rich people. They had, you know, they had the Cadillac, the big house, the motor boat, you know? The mother was really strict. Her discipline was outrageous. I see her as a psycho, basically.

While I was there I got into several different problems. There was two other boys and a girl; the two boys were eleven and thirteen and she was about nine years old. She wasn't a problem, but the two boys were monsters. And anything they did they now had a scapegoat. Here's this eight-year-old kid; he's new; he's stupid beyond belief, as far as caginess, or anything like that. Up till then, lying was simply … there seemed to be no purpose in it. Because there was no rules, there was no trouble you could get into. Therefore, there was no reason to avoid the truth, right? So this was where I really learned how to lie. These kids really did a good job of it. They showed me a lot of shit.

I got framed once. I was in bed sleeping. I don't know what time it was, but one of the boys flung open the door, turned on the light, points at me, just as his mother walks in, and he goes, look he's awake, he did it. And I'm like, what? What? What? And she started grilling me, saying that I had snuck into the livingroom and stole a chocolate bar, out of one of the bowls that they had there. I didn't even know what these bowls looked like. I got grilled and grilled and grilled until I couldn't take it any more, and I confessed. So I got my whipping and I went to bed. And on top of that I got all my candy taken away. I felt very hurt, of course. Like how could I be so stupid? But this happened several times. There was some dandy tricks that they pulled.

They killed birds and put them in the yard and said I did it. They'd break things and blame them on me. And I was getting really messed up. I remember that these situations often turned into anger, because of the fact that, you know, I felt that everybody was tricking me. I felt that I was being wronged constantly. Especially after the Cain family, I was an extremely angry person. I had been tortured, punished for things I didn't do, and there's nothing that bothers a person more. So, I was very angry. And whether or not I was out for revenge, I don't think so. I was basically living up to the expectations of the people who had punished me. Oh, I was a monster! I was throwing rocks, breaking windows. Anything that was built by man was my target. And I did some pretty spectacular damage at times. Just so methodical. I could break the same window fifteen, even twenty, times in a school or a building, right? You know, and like it. Because each time I'd come back to break the window, it would be a brand new one. But mostly it was just extreme anger, and it was hidden, deeply hidden within me. Yeah, nobody saw the anger. I would be laughing as I shattered the window.

I eventually had to leave that family. Welfare came and took me away. I was put in with another family, the Dales. They were Jehovah's Witnesses. And these were excellent people. It was a big family with nine foster kids. It was your *family* family. And in this family there was very few rules: If you go anywhere, let us know, so we're not freaking out about where you are, right? And be back before supper time, right? It was basically the type of place where you could grow up. But I didn't last long there, about one year.

Nothing happened at that place. It was just that the Blacks had come to adopt me. I was nine. They took me up to Fort St. John. At first everything was as sweet as honey, right? They really wanted to ease me into this situation. It was a completely new environment. It was bush, single-wide trailer, a tank for the water that they would bring in on trucks. It was really earthy stuff. At first there was hardly any chores for me to do. It was just, take out the garbage. And then, a couple of weeks later, it was take out the garbage and feed the horses. Then it was take out the garbage, vacuum the house, do the dishes, and feed all the animals. We had pigs, ducks, chickens, horses, cows, and goats. It got really wild. That was until I was fifteen. And I basically thought of myself as a work horse. That's why they adopted me, eh.

A few months after I turned fifteen, I just left. At first I was just a lost soul. I started hanging around with people that were quite a bit older, people that had lived the street life for some time, still on the street, still without direction. But they appeared to be so knowledgeable, so worldly, you know.

Scamming welfare for money was the first thing they taught me. It wasn't a conscious decision not to work; it was just taking free money. Then I got into petty theft, stuff like that. Just small time. The scamming the welfare part was put to an end in 1984 or '85. And after that it was work or die, you know?

I did everything, kitchen helper, cook, moving companies, different types of manual labour. I managed to do pretty good. But, I still had no idea of building the foundations for my life. Just day-to-day, paycheque to paycheque. Then during the summer of 1987, everything went to hell.

At the beginning of the summer, everything was going beautifully. I was in the job-entry program, and I was working at a large restaurant in town, and in another smaller restaurant. I had a common-law wife, and a baby girl. I was paying rent on a place, kind of a run-down motel. I managed to buy a few things and we had a bicycle, stereo, clothes, various other things, creature comforts. Then, it turned out that the guy that owned the motel was operating it illegally, and he split town. Right after that the place was condemned, and we were thrown out. My girlfriend and my daughter went to a women's shelter. During that same time, I lost my job. Then someone broke into my place and stole everything, everything I owned.

I got into a depression, because I couldn't seem to control anything any more. I'd lost my job, everything I owned, and me and my girlfriend were growing farther and farther apart. I went into a depression over that and I couldn't concentrate on getting a job or anything. The depression led to hard drinking. I was on the street, didn't have any place to go, no money, no job. I ended up in the psych ward of the hospital for nine days.

After I got out of there, well, the reason I got out of there is they couldn't see anything wrong with me. I seemed normal to them. I can't give up my emotions, so I tend to think objectively, rather than deal with my emotions. And, to them, I appeared completely normal, when, in fact, the only feelings I had were feelings of destruction. I just wanted to destroy. I remember telling my psychiatrist that the feelings weren't directed at human beings. I was violent toward mankind's things, the things that he's constructed, the garbage, the concrete, the steel, the glass. It was all garbage to me. And all I wanted to do was just destroy these things, and I wasn't sure really what my anger was involved with. I remember telling him that. I didn't want to hurt a person, but I do want to destroy things. I just want to grab a chair and just totally destroy a room and go into the next one and do the same thing, you know. I can't remember what he told me.

I ended up leaving there. And, from there I went back to drinking. I couldn't do anything. I couldn't get a job. I just could not formulate anything. I had to go to the bottle. That was the only thing that was simple enough that I could understand. Just simply opening a bottle and drinking it, and going to wherever the hell you go after you drink. Then I did some LSD.

Before I done the LSD, I climbed up in the mountains with a

buddy of mine. We had a sawed-off .22 rifle that we went up in the hills with to shoot. I didn't realize at the time what I was acting out. But I was shooting stop-signs. I even broke into a BC Tel repeater station, got inside this thing. I shot the outside of it a few times, and then I got inside and shot every phone in there. They had computer components all rigged up on the wall and I started shooting holes in that. And I tried burning the place. It's all steel, eh. There was some smoke damage, I guess.

And from there, after I caught up with my buddy (he left when the shooting started), I said to my buddy, Hey, where can I put this gun? Where can I hide this gun, we've got to get rid of it, right? He told me we could put it out in this orchard where he had another one stashed. On the way out there, we ended up going into town. That's where we did the acid. He did three double-hits; I did one double-hit, and we drank a bottle of Schloss Laderheim, and a smaller bottle of sherry. We were pretty wrecked.

We had a cab come and we went up into the orchard, and that's when things got really wild. I'm not even really sure of the details any more. The end result was, there was a man dead, the cab driver, and me and my buddy were driving away, driving into town. He was a total stranger. I know for a fact, I mean, I'm not a violent person, eh.

I was arrested eleven days after the shooting. After the trial was over and the jury went out, what was going through my mind was the absurdity of the fact that we were charged with first-degree murder. Also, I was thinking, any sane person listening to all the evidence, there's no way they could possibly come up with first-degree murder, you know? They couldn't possibly find us guilty. But when they did, it was almost as if it didn't surprise me. I became so detached when I heard him say "guilty as charged," it was like I was watching it on television or something. I was only dimly aware that it was me they were talking about, like a distant kind of a hazy thing.

It all seemed like a giant finger was just nudging me aside into a place where I couldn't get out. I don't know if I could ever, really, understand the sentence. Even if I was fifteen or twenty years into it already, I don't think I could really understand the sentence. It's not something tangible, it's not something that you can easily grasp. It's like they're saying, you are now void.

Twenty-five years, what is that? It's a deep space or something, right? It's not something you can actually visualize. When I envision the future, twenty-five years on the street is impossible to visualize. I'm not even too sure that I'll even know after a while whether I'm in prison or not. I feel in my mind that there's a good chance that I'll just completely lose my mind with boredom, or I'll die.

Like, my buddy didn't do anything, didn't hurt anyone, didn't, you know, he was peaceful, everybody liked him, but, just a few days ago, he got killed, just like that. Over nothing. That's a hard one to understand. He never had any idea that he was just going to be phased out like that. There's lots of things that can happen.

When I told them that I was guilty, I knew that I was taking a step into something that was real sinister, real dark, something that I was real tentative and scared about. It was like stepping over something that you couldn't step over. It was like your foot's reaching and reaching and reaching. And I took the plunge.

But the whole idea behind it was to learn, right? I came to prison with the idea that I put myself here because I needed to learn something. Well, it was big, bloody mistake, you know. There's nothing really to learn in here. I have learned. I've learned all the wrong things. I've learned that people can be influenced by the people around them in such a negative way. These people are all here for being criminals. You're surrounded by criminals. I mean, you hear about doing life on the instalment plan. There's these guys that do not want to change their ways no matter what. Some of them are forty, fifty years old and they've been into crime their whole lives. They've done my sentence already, in little bits. Five years here, seven years here, whatever. And I look at these guys and shake my head, and I'm going, if they had given me five years, I would have left here straight-joe, you know? I'm not kidding; I would have hit the street going, man, am I glad to be out. I'll never see the inside of that place again. And I know I wouldn't, because I would just say, hey, there's nothing I can do out here, short of stealing a million dollars and running, that would be worth going back there for. There's nothing outside for me, criminally, that would be worth coming back in here again. I've already seen it, I don't like it, and I'll stay out, thank you. But I was shafted right past that point. "I'm sorry buddy, we're not going to teach you a lesson, we're just putting you away; them's the breaks." I wanted to appeal, but Legal Aid won't pay for it, so I'm screwed. It's a total shaft here, man.

Life-10 is probably the largest sentence that really makes sense. And it's not just from the point of view of me, it's from the point of view of society too. The whole idea behind prisons is supposed to be rehabilitation. And that means it's like taking a part and repairing it.

There are some that just can't be helped, you know. I'm not real sure of that. The best place for them would be in a place where they might be able to help them. They're psychologically messed up, severely psycho, or really in bad shape. Whether they're like the beaten dog that's just been kicked around too damn much and has finally had it, he's not taking nothing from no one, or whether they've just, you know, slipped a cog somewhere in life, psychotic.

Those two types should be put in a mental institute of some kind to try and help them, to fix the problem. I mean, this person was in the machine of society, he was taken out, and before you put him back in, you've got to fix him, do something with him so when you put him back in the machine he's going to work. Not bang him and mash him up a little worse so when you throw him back into the machine he wrecks a bunch of other things, you know. You've got to try. Rehabilitation is fixing, fixing the broken piece, fixing the part that's not working properly. The whole idea of society, this machine, right, is fix the parts and the machine will work.

The object they've got now, is throw the part away. Let it rust and then maybe one day we'll put it back. It's all totally haywire. It's not a place where you can learn or fix yourself, it's a place where you've just got to sit and try to cope. How do I deal with the stress? That's tricky. It's a kind of thing where it's like a shellfish. I just hook myself onto the bottom of the ocean and let the currents kind of toss me this way and that way, but I'm hooked on nice and tight and trying not to let the insanity move me from my little rock. I smoke a lot. I mean, I smoke a *lot.* Drink coffee. Try to take my mind away by playing card games with other people, and listening to music. I watch some TV. Not a lot. I'm not really into TV that much. And that's about it.

Sometimes it's like a sardine. It's like taking twenty square blocks of houses and pulling all of those people out and sticking them into close quarters with you. The only difference between the people in prison and the people that are outside is the fact of where they are. I mean, sure there's people that don't break the laws on the street, but those people are actually pretty rare.

It's like speeding up your life twenty times. It's compact, faster. Everything happens right here, right now. I mean, it's very, very fast-paced. A day is: going ten blocks down, talking to your neighbour. Five minutes later, he's at your door talking to you; two seconds later you're passing by him on the street; five or six of your other neighbours just happen to be sitting on a lawn; you walk by, you talk to them, they talk to you, you sit down, do something with them. It's really, really fast-paced. You're moving, you're seeing these people instead of once or twice a day, you're seeing them ten, twenty, thirty times a day. And there's no real way of dealing with it. I mean, it's like, how do you deal with one of your days? It's the same thing, except for speeded up. You sit down after a rough day, put your feet up and relax for an hour or so, kind of let your thoughts sink in. Well, in prison, you would sit down and relax for three minutes. And then join the rat race again.

Do you know the difference between say, a bee that's doing his job and happy, as compared with a bee that has just stung someone and knows it's going to die, but is still clinging onto your skin, grinding its head into your arm, holding on tight? Well, the fury, the energy that's in your mind is like, a hundred times more than normal. Think, think, think, think. It's a furious thinking. Sometimes it's even deep thinking, the type of thinking where you sit back and really go into philosophy and stuff. But, most of the time, it's just like fury, like anger, like frustration. It's really fierce energy in your mind. But it's not really directed at anything in particular, just too many things banging into your brain, too many things trying to stimulate your mind. But it's all coming from inside you.

Out there on the street, it was like the fierce energy, your mind, was being put only towards staying alive. Here, your fierce energy in your mind is used to try to stay sane, to try to understand what the hell is this? This is lunacy? It's not, I mean for guys like me, it's not a place where you're taught a lesson. I mean, you give a guy life-25 and right there, he just goes phfft! There's my gigantic folder of life: flutter, flutter, out the window. You know there's no sense correcting the mistakes you made in that thing. I mean, you're not going to be able to open it up again, right? I mean, if you ever open it up again, you're forty-eight years old. Man, like, things out there are going to be so strange. It's like a deep freeze.

UPDATE

A follow-up interview was conducted with Mark in 1995 in which he talked about the stabilizing effect of staying in one place. By staying in Kent, rather than seeking a transfer to a less restrictive medium-security prison, he felt he could "sit and grow up, rather than just adapting constantly." When asked how he thought his thinking had changed, he suggested he was "more emotionally mature and more difficult to provoke, and not nearly as reactive to certain attitudes, perceived attitudes."

But since that interview much has changed. Mark was involved in an incident at Kent. He wasn't the instigator of the incident, but Mark was immediately identified as the accomplice and was taken to the punitive segregation unit (the hole). For the first few months there he seemed to be adjusting well, but then something went wrong. The details are sketchy but he apparently started throwing things (one source said billiard balls) at the guard post and became difficult to restrain. Whether this is indeed what happened is unclear, but the scenario immediately brought to mind the "fierce energy in [his] mind."

KURT

'Never been a storyteller, nothing to tell'

Kurt was twenty-three years old when sentenced to life-25. He had served two years at the time of his interview.

Growing up, I never really had a father. I've had a stepfather, but all he was there for was to pay the bills and be with my mother until my sister came into the picture. I have one brother, three years older than me, twenty-three right now. A younger sister, sixteen going on seventeen. Now, none of us are religious, like that. We were never close; it's more or less, we're there.

My mother's the oldest of eight kids and her mother was a single parent. All of the other kids in her family have been in trouble with the law, and she kept me, my brother, and sister away from my family. Like, I was seventeen years old when I first moved in with a few of them and found out what it was all about. I've always known who my uncles were, their names and that, but I've never known them. They were never over and we never went to visit; we were always isolated from names, faces.

It sounds kind of silly, but that's the way it is now that I look back at it. I have a lot of problems dealing with how I was raised, but it's all over now and I try to make do with the family support I have now.

I keep in touch with my family, weekly with phone calls, and about every week and a half, two weeks, I write a letter or receive a letter. They come in to visit, to the socials, usually every two months. I know that my mother understands what's happened in the past and wants to try to make up for that now, but it kind of hurts me a lot because it's kind of too late. Like, I'm here.

My brother, I've never really been close to him. I want to try. Even though I'm in here, I'm trying to get closer with him and my sister. It seems I can to talk to them now. And with the fact being that I'm in here, it's hard sometimes, but they understand. They've seen the problems that's led up to this, but we never really talk about it.

I was a compulsive shoplifter. I remember my brother being caught once at Safeway. Nothing criminal came out of that. I really don't know how I got started, I remember my brother used to baby-sit us, and I remember I used to beg him to go out to a corner store and, no money, I'd just walk in and steal whatever I could. I used to steal books, like binders for school. No reason. I don't know why. I was lucky actually that I was given probation time after time.

Then, I think when I was fifteen, late fourteen, I committed a B&E for the first time, our next-door neighbour's house. My mother was the one that phoned the police! She didn't know I was there. There was four of us; we skipped out from school and came back and these two guys were in the front of the street, just hanging around, and she thought something was up, so she watched. Me and another guy were in the back. She seen some legs going through a back window so she phoned, and a few minutes later, fifteen minutes later, a police car drove in our front driveway with me in the back.

I was sent to Maple Ridge Wilderness School. They have a nine-weekend program, nine weekends in a row. I completed that, and actually it was one of the better times I had in my life, because they're not really guards; they're, like, counsellors. It was rigorous, but you learn a whole bunch of things. Every three weeks you progress. First you're on level one, then two, then three. And on the last one, we go on a solo. They put us in the bush by ourselves for the whole weekend with nothing except a piece of plastic and a sleeping bag. I enjoyed that. I learned a lot.

Then, when I turned sixteen, actually I was fifteen, I was in for two shoplifting convictions. I was sentenced to the House of Concord. It was a probationary program, six months. It's a point program. You have to earn two sets of points, kind of like the wilderness program. You progress in levels and you get out when you get through.

I didn't want to leave there. When the time came, I was crying; that was my home. I was more free there than I was at home. They took us to Playland. I learned a lot, I met a lot of people. I grew really close to the counsellors there. I went to a couple of their houses, you know, and I didn't want to leave. It's run by the Salvation Army, and teenagers from all over North America go to this place, it's a million-dollar resort. Jervis Inlet, by Sechelt. It's the best time I've ever had in my life. I met so many people from all over. Movie stars used to go there in the thirties. Nothing can ever, I don't think can ever, top that, unless I was released one day. But, until then, that's it.

Then I went to Willingdon in '87. I spent three months in there for uttering a threat actually. I was watching the news hour at lunch time with my mom and a piece came on. My uncle was lying in the gunstore, shot with a shotgun at a place in Surrey. So, the next day I seen my mom, she was crying, and my grandmother was crying. He lost his thumb, and was shot in the abdomen. Everyone said he'd tried to rob it. I didn't know, I was just hurt because I seen my family and my mother was hurt.

So I went in there the next day. I skipped out of school. I went in there with a friend. At no time did I threaten this guy. All I did was ask him if he knew who my uncle was, and I knew he did. They knew each other way before I was born. He denied it. And then, my friend said, let's go, because the guy was looking very paranoid. I went to go to the door but it has automatic locks, and just like that, within thirty seconds, there were four or five police cars, and three news cameras from different places, and they took me in. I got six months for that. My longest bit. They said I was going to blow the store and shoot him.

I had just turned sixteen at this time, and I had witnesses, but the prosecutor stood up and said, if you can believe it, he said that if I'm not punished that I'll turn out like my uncles. So I was given six months.

I guess rebellion kicked in. So, when I got out, I had a discussion with my mother and I said that if things don't change, I'm going to get put in a group home or whatever, because it's not the life for me. Nothing changed. I was seventeen years old and I was home by six o'clock, no social life. So one night I just didn't come home. I never talked to her for a year until two weeks after I was arrested for murder.

During this time I moved in with various uncles. They were right into professional stealing. I bought my first vehicle, a van which we used for stealing plywood. They taught me how to do this, and how to buy insurance with no money, and the whole scam, smash and grabs from businesses. Actually, I enjoyed this. I enjoyed the money, and the thrill of the adrenaline rush. Things progressed; March of '88, I was involved in an armed robbery. I never actually had the gun, but I was in the store and we kept saying: You do it. No, you do it. I went in first, and I turned around and he had a gun on him! Holy cow, eh! No bullets or anything. Got eighty dollars, and then we ran for about two hours.

Finally got on a bus, and the bus driver stopped right in front of the store! I guess they had a bulletin out (I had a big, red ski jacket on). First we stopped outside a gas station. The bus driver told me he had brake problems and was going to stop and use the phone. When he came back from the gas station, he pulled off the road. We were down by the SkyTrain station down there, at 22nd or something. And about fifteen or seventeen police cars brought a gun in every window on the bus. Holy cow, you know!

I beat that in court. So I spent two months in jail for nothing while waiting to go to court, but I was kind of involved, so I didn't really gripe that. I got out, started drinking. One of my uncles got me hooked on cocaine. He was the one who testified against me in court. He got me an extra fifteen for the murder beef.

What happened was, I got out, started stealing, doing things, drinking. I went to the bar, just about every night. Go see where the strippers are, and then go to the cabaret. My lifestyle, from the time I left home, was, stay out till … well, wake up anywhere around noon or two o'clock in the afternoon. Go out, look for things to steal. What I would do, I would steal, like, thirty VCRs from one store in one week. I was getting ready to put on Woodward's coveralls and a dolly and pretend I worked there. It was good money.

Then I started getting ripped off by my family, my uncles. There was a lot of problems. I was ready to pack up and leave but I couldn't. Leave? I've never been anywhere really, like on my own, and I couldn't do it. It was the biggest mistake of my life other than what has happened, why I'm doing this interview. I would drink every night, and go out and steal with the relatives. And we'd go to the bar and sell things; work from six to eight all the way till closing time, one-thirty, two in the morning. Go back, stay up a while, high on cocaine, and wake up at twelve or two in the afternoon. Every day, the same thing.

One night, I was charged with murder, which happened at this other bar, strangulation. It was the most horrible thing that ever came across me. It's hard to grasp. It's over for now. I've never denied causing the death, but how it turned out was wrong. It was a wrong verdict.

I was on remand for seventeen months at Oakalla, and not once tried to prove my innocence, always remained guilty. But they held me for seventeen months, and then three weeks before trial they offered a second-degree deal, which means that I would be out in ten, parole eligibility at ten years. But because I was in custody for a year and a half, my review would come in eight and a half. I know what I did, but, like, it wasn't premeditated and it wasn't second-degree. It was a true case of manslaughter, and I wasn't going to compromise. If I knew I committed first-degree murder and they offered me second, that's a fifteen-year difference, I would have taken it. Both lawyers told me not to plead. So, I said, okay, I wasn't going to.

I phoned up a very good friend of mine, and one of my uncles was there. He wanted to talk to me. He's been friends with the victim's family since before I was born. I told him about the offer. He told me that I should plead guilty to second-degree and save everyone the hassle of going to court; he knows what's right for me. I said no, and the next day, he was a Crown witness. He says that I told him exactly thirty days before any of this happened I was going to go hunt this person down. It's very ludicrous.

I can't believe that his evidence was admissible in court. He has a long record. My lawyer held up my uncle's record, and my lawyer is six-two, and he held it over his head and it still hit the ground. And since being here in Kent, I've talked to people who know him. He has ties with the police. Something happened in RPC [Regional Psychiatric Centre] in '86, that ended in a murder. My uncle testified, and he got stabbed seven times as a result of that. I think he makes a little bit of money doing it. If I had told him I was going to do this, it wouldn't have bothered me that much, but he lied and used the family name against me – the family tie – and that's wrong.

Anyway, the deliberation took five and a half hours. The whole court case took only two weeks, and during the deliberation the jury came back and wanted to know the difference between second-degree and manslaughter. So right there, you know, my mind went to work. I was kind of disappointed that there was no verdict because I had to prepare for all that. It took a lot from me. Another two, two and a half hours, I came back and the jury was smiling at me when they came in for the verdict.

The foreman of the jury, he looked at me and smiled … you know, I took that as, a fair judgment's coming. And, when they said "first," my knees went rubbery. I wanted to cry. I couldn't cry. The judge asked me if I had anything to say. I wanted to say some mean things, some smart-ass comments, but I just said, "Not at the present time, your Honour." That was it. I didn't want to turn around and look at the people who were supporting me from behind. I don't know. I just went back. Couldn't believe it. My life passed by my face, my life.

I tell you, I was terrified! I talked to a lot of people trying to find out about this place, about Kent. And I tried to get my transfer put off. You have thirty days if you don't sign a waiver, and I never signed it, so I got a stay for thirty days. It was like before I went to the juvenile place, I was terrified too. You hear things, you see things on TV, bad boys. And you go to see movies. When I went to Oakalla I was petrified too. I just got arrested for murder. You know, I'd never been in adult before. I'm young. You hear things about young guys, you know? So, I didn't know what to do.

I phoned the federal classification office to say that I had to stay close to Vancouver to speak to my lawyer. He said he would do it for me. But then the envelope came, and I was on the bus to Kent.

There were eight guys on the bus, and they're all [General] Population, but they put us together and no one knew where the others came from, so I didn't say anything. I just pretended I was one of the boys, right? They took us to Matsqui Institution first. I remember I went to Matsqui once when I was a juvenile and we were dropping somebody off, so I knew what it looked like. They took me inside, handcuffed, shackled – it's not a good feeling for anybody. They strip-searched me. They didn't really need to. Anyways, I was put on a different van, a Corrections vehicle, by myself, and driven over to Kent.

It looked really weird. It was not what I imagined. I thought it was going to be all bars, like something like Alcatraz or something. I had no idea what it looked like. I came in and I seen people with TVs and stereos and pictures on the walls and, no bars. Like, no bar bars. Just, in the windows, these two big tubes. And doors, solid doors, with one little window. And, you know, it really made the transition easy.

The people in here, they're more … they don't play the hard con game. It's more or less, we're all here, let's make it as best as possible, you know? Now, it's like I've been here for a long time. It's like, this is my home. It is. People who say otherwise are full of shit. You're going to be in here longer than anywhere else.

I have been sent a lot of lifer literature from the government in Ottawa, and when I read it, I make light of it, kind of, with other guys, you know. I can't imagine being down all the time, because we are here, we're not going anywhere. We have to face it, so why not really have fun and joke about it, because what happened is serious, and I don't think anybody should have to have this happen. But we have to kind of keep our heads up.

But the twenty-five years. A lot of people say, I don't give a shit. What can they do to you, throw you in jail? But I have a lot still. I have myself. I'd rather be here than locked up twenty-four hours a day, or twenty-three hours. I don't want to get in any trouble, because I have that fifteen-year judicial review. If my appeal fails, that's still there. I still have that to cling onto. Not to mention there's schooling here. I want to obtain whatever I can in here, and I'm very mad at myself, I guess, because I didn't realize how important an education was.

I thought school was a drag. I never really thought it would mean very much because I loved the life of stealing and all that. I didn't really care. I skipped out. I couldn't really sit down in school. I wasn't sociable. Like, I've always been level-headed, you know? I'm not ignorant or arrogant, but I never liked the groups.

All the way up to Grade 7, I had very good marks, but I guess that's common. Grade 8, I had extreme difficulty; Grade 9, same thing, got kicked out of four high schools for skipping out. When I left home at the beginning of '88, I signed up for the February semester, the second semester, and I went for three weeks. But because of all my other priorities, I couldn't handle the staying up late and going to school, and it just didn't mean anything. But in that time, I had the best marks of my high school years. I was taking trades maths, and other courses. I was proud of myself for that time.

Now, even though I'm in, I have to look at it that I'm here for twenty-five years, nothing less, so whatever comes really is a bonus, you know. Most people think, well, who needs an education? But, when you're around the same people all the time there's nothing to talk about. The more I learn, the better I feel about myself, and the better I get along with other people. I guess it's just … just life, I guess. But it's kind of easier now. I guess I'm a bit maturer, smarter. I can look at everything now and see what it means, how to under-stand it, how to apply it. It's just too bad it's too late.

I'll probably stay at Kent for two years before I apply for a trans-fer, like until my appeal's over. Everybody, most of the inmates, told me here and when I was in Oakalla that before I go anywhere else, I'll have to go to RPC's violent offenders program. I've seen my CMO [Case Management Officer] here and he told me that I would probably go to somewhere like a medium, like, Mission or Moun-tain, before I go there, which doesn't really matter to me as long as I don't stay in one place for the whole twenty-five years. If that's what it stays at, I want to see it broken up.

When I first got arrested, I was put in population and was in there just under a month, but then there were articles in the newspaper, people spreading rumours. My victim was a woman, so they say rape, and skinner, and woman-killer, but there was no rape. I never raped anybody. A sexual encounter did happen, but it was proven by a doctor that there was no signs of any force. But I decided I'd better protect myself and check in [ask for protective custody].

In a way it's not much different in PC. I feel there's less games. There's the people like, there's the rats. Those are the people who always hang around the office. Doesn't matter whose skin it costs, they'll do whatever they can to benefit themselves. There are people who think they're big or want to be big. Sometimes they create problems. But, I'm surprised that there's so little of that here. I thought it was going to be worse than juvenile, and it's a hell of a lot better. There's none of this muscle action going on, but there's a few bugs, and when I say bugs I mean people that are mentally disturbed. They shouldn't be here. There are, like, people that are really bad, but as long as they don't hurt anybody I love or care about, I don't care. It sounds kind of cold, but, it's just the way it is.

I keep away from the guards here, not because I hate guards or people in uniform, but because problems do arise. When I need something, like if I have to make a phone call, or have to get this or get that, then I'll go down there. I don't have any bad rapport with any of the guards, except with maybe one, but nothing serious. No bad words. I just keep to myself a lot. I enjoy my solitude time. And with a roommate in here, it's very hard. But when I get it, I use it.

The roommate I have now is the third one since I've been here. He's the best roommate I've had so far. I like him. He's like, just over twice my age, but he's done a lot of time. He's spent just about his whole life in here, and because I'm young it's kind of like I don't know anything. I agree I don't, but sometimes it's hard. It's like, everywhere I go on the street, I'm always told what to do. In here, the guards tell us what to do, but when it comes to, you know, other people, it gets frustrating. After you've been together a while, you pick out, just like anywhere else, just like if you were married or whatever, you pick out things that irritate you. But, right now, it's pretty casual.

But because I do like my quiet time, I stay in my house, my cell, most of the time. After a while, a few months or whatever, people know if you're all right or not. You form little social circles. You communicate with these guys, say hi to them. Like, I have no qualms with anybody, no serious problems with anybody in my unit. But there's a few people, I think, you know, under my breath, you know, I don't really like him, but, oh hi, how are you doing? Hey, you have to. I've never been the type of person that … I'm non-violent I guess. I've never wanted to end up in fisticuffs. You stay away and most of the time, people respect that.

A typical day? Well Monday to Friday, I try to get to sleep right after lockup, which is about eleven o'clock. I try to have the TV and everything off by twelve, because I do work. I don't like not having enough sleep, I'm grouchy. I work in textiles, making clothing to supply other jails across Canada — underwear and shirts — and I enjoy it. I'm one of the senior people there I guess now. I enjoy the work as it breaks up my day. I get to be around different people from different units and, I guess, get away. Go back, have lunch, come back and work. Three afternoons a week I attend school — SFU. Mondays I have psychology. Tuesdays and Fridays I have GED. Every day, Monday to Friday, I look forward to getting back to three o'clock lockup. Mail comes at that time. Mail cheers me up. I write several people around the world; means a lot to me. I have some very close friends, considering they've never had a picture of me, and we've never seen or talked to each other. It's quite unusual to say the least, but it means a lot to me, these people.

We eat around three-thirty, three-forty-five. Then I look forward to gym. It breaks up the day also. Like I said earlier, I'm very active in sports. Then we get back at six from the gym and pretty well sit around from six till lockup. Now it's hockey season, and I just love the NHL. It's going to fill up a lot of my time. And that's what it's all about is using your time to the fullest. Education. Using everything they give you in here to your advantage.

I'd like to see more unity between all the lifers groups. Like, get money-making ventures happening. I'd see that we have things to do so we don't sit around and say, screw this, or fuck this. That's not doing anything. With a lifers group, once a month we're allowed to have take-out orders from the outside. That's all right. And we have guest speakers that come in. The last one we had was a German. I forget, not a psychologist, something religious. Like some -ology or other. Yeah, like theology. Yeah, and like totally German. The CSC hired this guy from Germany! They paid him all this money, to talk to lifers and people in jail across Canada. And, like I didn't think of this until someone else brought it up, but why would they pay … they paid more money to this guy because he's from far away. Why not hire someone here? Are they not capable enough or something? That's sad, that's prejudice to me, and they hire this old guy that runs CSC, from Denmark! Yeah! I can't believe it! I'd rather get transferred over to Denmark. I heard it's better over there. These people don't know anything about us.

I want to see like, organized things. Like things that happen here, they're so unorganized; they say we can have a meeting once a week, and we've been having them for the whole time I've been here, just about every other week. They say: you guys aren't having lifers meetings; we haven't heard anything about it. It's games, eh, and they do it purposely. They try to get it stopped because they don't want everybody together, because when everybody's together, we get more things, and they don't want that. But I can't understand that, because there'd be less problems. It's been shown already. If we have things to do, people will be more careful and cautious, not to get into that fight, or do something wrong. It just doesn't make sense to me. But that's the foreign people for you, I guess.

This is like a little town, isolated, and when they come to accept that, I guess, things will be more appropriate. The rehabilitative outlets here? There are none. And it's really astounding because since I've been here, half the people that I've met are parole violators.

They come to Kent, and they get released from Kent. But they have no programs for that. That really shouldn't affect me, but it does.

When I see these people not getting psychological help they need, the outside support, the transition from being in here to out there, and just coping. When they don't get any of that, it bothers me because somebody could get hurt for no reason. And it is a waste of taxpayers' money having these people brought in when they could be dealt with in another way. It's just a waste of money and it destroys people's lives, souls, I guess.

I always wondered why people were so quick-tempered in here. I was never like that. But within the last few months, the administration changed here, got manipulative towards us. Like, I have nothing to do with them. I do my programs and I'm not any problem whatsoever, but they still affect me in a way they shouldn't affect me. Like, games. My anger has risen. I get angry quick for no reason. And it makes people violent in here, not inmates against inmates, but … it's incredible. And they wonder why people keep coming back, and doing more violent crimes, and it's really sad to see because unless they do something now, they're going to have a hell of a problem. I guess they can keep building new jails.

So many things can be done. There's a lot of people in here who shouldn't be here and it's really sad to see. It hurts me. Some people I wish would never get out because, you know, I still have people out there that I care about. It's not nice to say, but you have people who are only doing a few years who are dangerous, it's not until you're around them that you know.

UPDATE

Kurt was transferred to Mountain Institution in the summer of 1994. At first he wanted to go back to Kent, but has since settled in. He saw taking the violent offenders program at RPC as "the best thing I ever did in life." He pointed out that CSC policy was changing and that an inmate no longer had to spend close to ten years at Kent before going to RPC (he went after five years). He felt that he had actually grown up as a consequence of that period at RPC. He had cut off all contact with his family, "shut everybody out," since he now realized that what he had once thought was "normal" was anything but. When the "incident" occurred he had been, in his estimation, "a child mentally." He now discussed in detail how the death of the young woman had come about. He had "never been a storyteller, nothing to tell." He talked about the loneliness he experienced growing up, "because of my family," and how "loneliness is a killer in itself." Until RPC he felt that he'd lived his life "underwater;" now he was "above" and in the last few months had been able to see so many things. "Now I'm starting to like who I am, but how could I have done that. I'm not an animal, but what I did was like an animal." He carried around, at all times, what he'd done, though some days he would "tuck my head in the sand and forget about it." He thought he needed to do more time still, "to get the hidden anger out," and is looking forward to doing the RPC program again. He'd finished his GED at Kent and was in the midst of a first-level psychology course when the SFU Prison Education Program had been cancelled. All the talk about taking away the judicial review had set him back several months, but he was now able to think about the future in a more optimistic light: "I have so much hope inside."

JOHN

'They count you like diamonds, and treat you like shit.'

John was thirty-eight when sentenced to life-25. He had served two and a half years at the time of his interview.

I've only been in one provincial joint and I've been to a few remand centres. This is the first federal place I've ever been in. Kent is … well, you can make more of a home here when you know you're going to be doing a long time. These provincial joints, where you're sentenced to just a few months, you are just thrown into a cell; no TV, no radio or anything like that, and you're just put there, and you're just there for a few months; a short time, so it's pretty much like warehousing. Here you can kind of make your own little home. I found the food better in the provincial joints – much better.

Actually it was a federal/provincial joint, so you had both. You had federal guys in there who were coming off long bits and a lot of guys in there doing thirty days, three months, six months, like that. The food was very good I thought for a joint. That was my first time ever having been in jail, other than the remand centres. Here, the food is really bland. You never look forward to going to any meals. Once or twice a year we get steak and that's a big happening. A little wee scrawny steak and that's a big deal. It sounds funny to somebody outside, but when you're in here and you only get it once or twice a year, it's a big thing. The rest is dog food.

Well, there's not too much in the way of sports. There's not too much here to do. I'm forty now so I, like I lift weights now, eh. I work out lifting weights. I'll play a little volleyball whenever a volleyball game is on. I've been into floor hockey, play a little softball. I've gotten into that. Mostly I stick with working out, eh.

I've been in for two and a half years, just about going on three years. Seems like forever already. It's hard to remember what it's like out there. So many things can happen in three years. It's a terrible transition period; it's a terrible thing to go through. Especially, when you don't see a light at the end of the tunnel anywhere. You're just stuck here and you're herded into your cell every few hours for a count. You feel like cattle. You get a feeling like you're helpless. Herd you in, lock the door. They count you like diamonds and treat you like shit.

Well, my mother was on welfare because my father was killed when I was six. She had a part time job in a dry-cleaners in town and she got welfare too, to support four kids, eh. So we grew up all our life with a real low budget. I had an allowance of twenty-five cents a week when we were kids, and we were lucky to get that. It was kind of rough growing up in that respect. Although, now when I think back, it was a good environment, you know.

My mother died when I was seventeen. She died of cancer. Then it was just a year and a half later that I got married. I got married in September, we had a baby in October. It lasted a couple of years. Like, I was just a kid and so was she. And we just kind of dwindled apart. And then I did a lot of work with carpet factories, laying carpets, working in the warehouse. And I've been on all kinds of construction jobs.

I got two brothers. One's been in the Air Force for over twenty years now. He shot himself in the head last Christmas, back in Ontario, but he's alive. I hadn't spoken to him for over ten years until this happened, when I found out about it. Now I'm writing to him back and forth. He's at an Air Force hospital base. So, I correspond with him now and he's still trying to recuperate. I guess his physical injuries are okay now, it's just a little mentally hard on him. He's going through a rough time. His wife and him just broke up after being married fifteen years. My oldest brother and my younger sister, they're the reason I'm here, and I don't know what I feel towards them. I just don't know.

My sister worked at secretarial work all her life. She's going to be thirty-seven years old in May. She works for the Forestry and the last time I'd seen her or talked to her she'd been working for Workmen's Compensation for three or four years, as a secretary. My brother, he's a painter, you know a house painter. He's been doing that since he was a kid. Married, three kids. My sister's single, never been married.

The prosecution said my sister and brother called Crime Stoppers and said that they know of somebody that killed a guy nine years earlier, and they named me as the guy that did the murder. And so they picked me up and they charged me. I sit in, like, the remand centre for ten months. I go through my preliminary, my sister takes the stand and says this one night, ten years ago, I came over to her house and said I had just finished coming from committing murder and I cut this guy's throat and stabbed him. She says that I came over that night and just told her this and I was shaking, visibly upset, and hyper. She was the main witness. And my brother says that months later I told him that I'd cut a guy's throat and killed him and he'd dropped like that. Like, that was their evidence.

They took me to trial on that and it was my story against my sister's story, and brother. The prosecution claimed that I arranged to meet this guy and we met, and went to an apartment building, like in the basement, and he was grabbed from the shadows by the two other people, and that his throat was cut from ear to ear and he was stabbed twenty-seven times. And they say that I actually did the killing myself or aided and abetted the actual murderers. They didn't know for sure.

The whole thing was hearsay and circumstantial. And, like, that was their basic evidence. And it was just my luck at having the rottenest lawyer I could ever imagine having. He just didn't ask the right things or he didn't delve into my sister's background, that she's a flake, been seeing psychiatrists and psychologists for as far back as twenty years ago, where she is notorious for blowing everything that has developed around her life out of proportion. She blows everything out of proportion.

I said I went over to my sister's house one night, I said it was a month or a month and a half after the murder had been committed, and I said that the only time I talked to my sister about this murder was when I got the newspaper and it had a story about this guy that had been found in a car and that he had been stabbed and that, so on and so forth. And I showed her that because the guy was an alleged killer who was living with my ex-wife. So that's sort of how I started talking to her about it. They thought maybe jealous husband or words like that. My sister now after all these years, I don't know if she's … like in her mind, she's imagining that I came over and told her that I just killed a guy.

She says she was too afraid to say anything at the time, afraid for her life. She says I told her that if she ever said anything about it, that like this friend of mine would take care of her, which is totally absurd, you know, because we've been so close for these past ten years that, ah, you know where she says she's been scared for her life? Her and I have been so close. I've taken care of her like a big brother, or else like a father and all of a sudden, boom, she goes, I can't live with these feelings anymore – I've got to tell somebody. And then she phones up Crime Stoppers. And she got this story all laid out, her and my brother together.

My brother had a reason to do something against me, because he knew I'd had an affair with his wife seven or eight years ago, and this was his way of getting even with me. I know him; he's a prick; he's an asshole. They concocted the two stories together. Like I feel it was my brother that urged my sister to believe that I did this killing, whereas I told my sister when I went over to her place that night and showed her the newspaper clipping, and I was going like, Bob Jackson stabbed all those times and I said it must have been horrible, and just talking like that, because she knew him too, eh.

When my lawyer asked my brother on the stand, he says, why are you now coming forward after ten years and saying this about your brother? And his answer was, he said for no special reason, I'm just coming forward, you know. Like he denied knowing that his wife and I had had an affair when they were separated and he denied that's not the reason he's doing this to me. He said I don't know anything about an affair. And my sister, well, you could tell when she was on the stand, she's a flake. But my lawyer didn't bring out all this stuff about her seeing psychologists and psychiatrists for years and years, having nervous breakdowns and, ah, like he didn't delve into anything like that. And she just sat in the stand there all teary-eyed and kind of crying.

The jury they must be thinking, well this girl can't be lying about her brother. And I'm sitting there in this little box, and they're look-ing at me in this box and, like, I'd say that 90 percent of them are thinking, You're guilty anyways because you're charged with this crime, and your family's up there saying it's you. So there was a lot of that that goes on in their minds. Like I say, I had a four-day trial with all flimsy, flimsy evidence, just all hearsay and circumstantial, and the jury was kept five days deliberating – so there must have been an awful lot of doubt in there.

I was convicted and sentenced all in the same breath. I thought I was in a dream. And, like I was waiting to wake up. It didn't seem like it was me on trial there. I sat there for nine days, it was a four-day trial and five-day jury deliberation. And I sat downstairs in a tiny room for five days solid, from nine in the morning to ten at night, waiting for a jury to come to a verdict. It was the worst time in my life. They were the longest days, because every two minutes I'm knocking on the door asking the guard, what time is it?

You sit with no magazines, nothing. You just have a little bench to sit on. You can't even lean back; you just have to sit erect. Then you have to bang on the door for the guard to bring you a bale of tobacco and then he rolls one for you. And you just sit − five days, thirteen hours a day. It was hell. And then getting the worst news possible.

I was all built up because the guards were saying to me, after two or three days of jury deliberation, if they haven't come back with anything, you're either going to get a hung jury, or else you're going to get an acquittal. So by day four I was starting to feel a little more confident, and then the fifth day. I was just hoping for, you know … when your life is put into somebody else's hand, you just hope for the best.

I remember when they called me and advised me that, okay, they've come to a verdict. They walked me upstairs, took the cuffs off and put me in the courtroom. I sat down and then they said stand, when the jury was coming back. And the moment they walked in I knew that it was going to be guilty. Not one of them looked at me and they all had a solemn look on their faces. And then the jury foreman stood up and says, we find him guilty as charged, and in the same breath, the judge told me stand up again, it's a mandatory sentence, so I was sentenced to life imprisonment with no chance of parole for twenty-five years. He said that's a decision made up by Parliament and there was nothing he could do about it and that was it. And they took me away.

I still haven't come out of the shock. I still don't feel like it's happened to me. I'm here, but I feel I shouldn't be here. They had no evidence at all. It was a hearsay case. My lawyer was terrible. It was all just a bunch of mumbo-jumbo and like that got me where I am here.

But I waited thirty days. I didn't sign my papers for thirty days. I stayed in the pretrial for thirty days after the sentencing. You had the option where you could stay thirty days, where you could kind of get your stuff together. So I stayed there for thirty days, in total shock, not knowing what it was going to be like in a federal prison. I was thirty-eight when I was sentenced and you know I never thought all my life what it would be like. Watching television, you know, and you see these old prison shows and you think everyone's a 300-pound, bald-headed guy with tattoos on his head. You just don't know what you're walking into; it's like going into the dark and everything's unknown. It's like starting a new life in a different world.

The first night they brought me in at seven o'clock at night, so they didn't put me into population until the next morning because everything was closed up in the office. So they put me in a seg cell overnight. I didn't sleep a wink. The next morning they led me out into the population and I didn't know what it was like. I was scared of the unknown; a lot of fear, you know. A fear of everything – just anything, everything in general. I just had a terrible feeling. It's still there, but I've mellowed out as I've been here a couple of years.

Luckily I knew four or five guys from the ten months I spent in the pretrial centre before I come here. They put me on a unit where I knew a couple of guys, fortunately, so they helped me out at first, showed me where things were, you know, where you go to supper, where you go to pick up your clothes and things, so I had a little help that way. That first month, it was just trying to adjust to the lifestyle here. Like, when it's four-thirty supper time, everyone makes a beeline for supper and in the morning they open at quarter after seven it's for breakfast – everything is on a schedule, on a strict schedule in here. And, it's hard to explain, it's really hard to explain.

The doors open here around seven-fifteen to seven-thirty in the morning. Get up, wash up, get dressed, go to breakfast. And then right at eight o'clock they call everybody to work. Myself, I work in the library and I don't start until twelve-thirty, so I go back to my unit and either lie down and have a nap or sit around with a couple of the guys, drink coffee, talk, watch TV, write a letter, read a little bit. Then at twelve-thirty … well, like at twelve o'clock you go for lunch and then at twelve-thirty everyone is called back to work and you work until three o'clock. At three o'clock we go back to our units, sit around with the guys for a few minutes, get your mail, sit around talk till around three-thirty, when we're locked up for count. That's twenty minutes, sometimes half an hour. Doors usually open around four o'clock then you sit around, watch TV, boring routine. Four-thirty you go for supper, five-fifteen, everyone's called back to the units and we sit around, watch TV, shoot pool, do whatever little things there are to do on a little unit, but there's nothing to do but sit, watch TV or talk. Because you're locked in there.

At six o'clock there's a five-minute movement. Two to three nights a week I work in the library from six to seven, so I shoot down to the library, do whatever I have to do for an hour, then I go work out for an hour with a friend of mine, then it's back to the unit, have a shower, and then from there on I just watch TV, play cards. Doors are locked at eleven o'clock at night. Myself, I stay up and watch TV, usually until about two in the morning and then off to bed. And it's the same thing, over and over and over. Basically you just try and blank your mind from this place if you can. It's almost impossible to do. I find the best part of the whole day is at eleven o'clock at night when they lock the doors, when you can be in your cell by yourself and you know you're in there for the night and you can just lay back and think and relax. For me when I lay back at night, I start to think of things I used to do on the street and how great things were, and how bad some other things were. Just about what it was like out there, and that. At times I find it hard to really remember what a lot of things were like out there. It seems like it's been so long. It gets very depressing.

It's the waking up every morning and you're in a different world.

But you're here and there's no leaving it. Especially if you're doing life-25. You don't know when or if you're going to get out. You wonder if you're going to die in here. Your first shot, as it is now, is fifteen years and that's just an if, a maybe. Like you just don't know. I see guys in here that are doing life-10, but they've already got fourteen years in and they're no closer to getting out than the first day they got here. It's crazy, utterly crazy.

School? On the outside? Well, I didn't finish, like I quit in Grade 10. I liked school; I used to enjoy going to school. Back then, life seemed so much easier than today. I was kind of a rang-a-tang kid, small town, you know, we were always getting into trouble. Minor things. You know, stealing a pack of gum out of the store and end up having the storekeeper chase you around town, you know, little things like that. There wasn't much to do in a small town. So, I was always in little bits of trouble when I was a kid. And I got into trouble when I was in Grade 10 and I quit school.

I was charged with trying to break into a pool hall, with a friend of mine. And they caught us and they gave me the option of either going back to school, or getting a job, or going to reform school. I ended up getting a job.

I had been to reform school when I was fifteen, after me and my next older brother had had a fight with my mother's boyfriend and we ended up beating him up. It was a stupid thing, like we were on probation, and had to be in the house by nine o'clock, and we came in a couple of hours late one night and he was drunk. He was a big fat slob and he took a swipe at my brother, so I took a swipe back at him and a fight broke out and we ended up giving it to him real good.

We ran away, and three days later they picked us up and they took us to court and charged us with incorrigibility. So I went to Brandon Lake Reform School on Vancouver Island for a few months. Like, I was fifteen years old. I never hit jail, not even a city bucket, or anything, until I was about thirty-four, thirty-five years old. I always remembered that stay and I hated every second of it I was in there. Like, three months seemed forever.

The fifteen-year review? Well, you know what, I don't even think about that. I take it one day at a time. Like, if I think about tomorrow, it's just, tomorrow's Thursday. I don't even think about what I'm doing tomorrow. I'll wait till it comes. If you start looking ahead, even if you start looking ahead to tomorrow, or the next day, that's when you really feel the jolt of the time you have to be here. I try to go through the day without thinking of being here twenty-five years; I think it's so utterly ridiculous, twenty-five years; it's crazy, it's forever.

I try to think back twenty-five years to when I was fifteen. God, I try to recover a couple of memories from there, and then I think forward to twenty-five years in the future, and then I start getting screwed up, thinking crazy thoughts, so just try to put it out of my mind, and just try and get through my day. The only way I'm going to get through this.

Right now my mind seems like I'm doing remand time. My appeal should be happening soon. It's been almost two years now. All I've heard from the appeal board is that they're going to hear my appeal, but no dates yet. I have to wait for the appeal board to set the date. When you're here and they know you're here, your stuff gets stuck at the bottom of the pile. They know you're not going anywhere. The people who are running bail and stuff, they're at the top of the list. I'm not complaining; everyone goes through it. It's a long waiting game. You have to sit back and think, Well my turn's going to come up and hope for the best.

I try not to get too close to people I know are getting out soon. I have a few friends that I'm kind of close to. You can start hanging around with someone who sounds like a nice guy, and you start hanging out with him and then he's out within a year. I've had a couple of guys leave already and you can get to the point when you don't want to meet any more people. They come and they go and they come and they go, and you don't want to have anything to do with them.

But still you have to. There's twenty-four guys in each unit and six on each range, so I get kind of close to the guys on the range. There's a couple of guys who are getting out on Friday who've only been here for the last year. I'm happy for them going and I'm going to miss them. You get used to the guys around here … you meet them in the morning and you ask them for a cigarette and they'll sit down and talk to you for a few minutes, and then poof, he's gone, like he never existed here. There's another one going next month out of my unit and then my best friend is leaving next June. I dread those days coming. Not for the guys but for myself. I dread them going because you have to start all over again with someone else.

But I'm not hanging around with anyone else in here that's doing life. Like a lot of them are displaced anywhere. You have 140 or 150 inmates in population. When you go outside on a Saturday afternoon for a couple of hours to catch some sun – it's a beautiful, beautiful day, and there might be twenty-five people out there. So there's over a hundred people staying in their units, and a lot of them are lifers. There's about sixty here doing life. I done a count one day when I seen a list, and like there were thirty in population and thirty in PC. That was about a month ago, but since then there have been a couple of incidents. So there's like twenty-five in population.

I find that they just don't come out. I like to feel that I'm going out there to get a tan and it feels like you're laying in the park, like on the street. You shut your eyes and put your suntan lotion on and lay back and try to picture yourself getting a suntan and then you drift off a little bit. Sitting in a cell and staying by yourself all the time is too depressing. You get into a rut and then you don't know how to get out of the rut. But here, I don't know what it is with a lot of these guys, they just don't go outside. But that's how it is here; it's like being on hiatus from life. It's an indefinite hiatus.

Life in the units? I'm lucky I guess because I'm in a real quiet unit. There are a few guys in there roughly around my age and like there's no young kids with the music blaring who you have to go and tell them to turn it down every five minutes. I mean there's a lot of guys been killed in here for having their TV on too loud. They keep it on loud after lockup and the guy wants to sleep next door and they can argue when the guy tells them to shut the fucking TV off or else shut it down. And the guy says, fuck you, and then the other guys says, okay, I'll see you in the morning. Next morning the doors open up and the guy's in there with a shank, or he's beaten with a club or whatever.

I think when people come here, I think they kind of know in the back of their head that they just got to be cool. They got to respect people; like, you won't get any respect if you don't show any. And like I say, there are a lot of people who just don't come out and mingle with anybody. They go to meals and they go to work. You kind of blank them out. You don't want anything to do with them. And like I can't speak for everybody, but I just know how it is with me. Like, I'll say hi to most everybody in here. I'll say good morning while we're passing, but like I say, I'm sick of meeting people. I've met so many in the past two and a half years; a lot of good guys and a few assholes too, eh. But you stay clear away from them, eh. You learn to kind of weed them out and, like they say, there are 140 to 150 guys in here, I'll walk around or go lay out in the sun with maybe four or five different guys in the whole place, and sort of get a little close to them. Other than that, you know, I stay friendly with everybody. If the guy's an asshole, I'll stay away from him. There are a lot of good guys here. They treat you how you treat them. That's how I find it in here, but you do definitely wonder about everybody in here.

I mean, I sit in the kitchen sometime eating supper. I'm sitting there and I'm watching the line that's coming in, and you always look for the new faces coming in and see if you know anybody, or, if it's like a new face in the crowd – a fish – you see how they get treated. Because I remember the day that I came in; the first time I went to the cafeteria and I could feel a hundred sets of eyes on me. I could see everybody wondering who you are, what you're in for, how long you're doing. And now I find myself doing that, when I'm sitting there and the new people come in. You definitely wonder about everybody's beef. You don't go around asking, you just don't, but you hear a lot from other people. Most of the time I don't want to hear.

It would almost be like being out on the street, living in a neighbourhood, with a couple of hundred people; you don't know them, like we don't know everything about them, like you say hi to them in passing, but you may not know your neighbour for years and years and you live next door to them, eh. In a way, it's kind of similar in here. You know them, you say hi to them and that's about as far as you want it to go. I try to keep a pretty low profile. You know, I don't get involved in any cliques, you know with a bunch of dopers or anything. But if there's some smoke around, I'll smoke a joint or two.

I don't know if it's my age or what, but when I go back into my cell I'll sit and watch TV or lay back and think, or else I'll write a letter or something, but I won't get into the pigs' faces, and they don't get in mine, and I like it like that. I think with someone that stays away from them it makes them wonder what this guy's all about. But I just don't want to get involved with them. I heard that when you get down to lower security, like Matsqui or Mission, they're at you all the time with little things. Like you got to get up in the morning there at Matsqui and Mission. Here you don't have to get up for work; you don't have to go to school. There are a couple of guys in here who were at Matsqui doing short bits, three years, and they had a bunch of PNs. Like, they're not waking up in the morning to go to work and, boom, they shipped them here. And they like it much better here because they don't have to put up with all that crap. You know, the more you stay out of their faces, and stay away from arguments with them and that, the faster the time seems to go by. And, you know, you have to try to make it as pleasant as you can while you're here. So I just stay away from them. If I need a razor blade, I go ask for a razor blade. But other than that …

On the outside? I don't know. That's something you don't even really think about. I just take it one day at a time. I've been corresponding with a girl from out in Winnipeg now for over a year and she's talking about she'd like to get married and that. So I think if I got out tomorrow morning, I'd start up a relationship with her out there. I mean it's so different from here. Here it's a paper relationship. I'd try and start up a relationship with her. I'd probably move in with her and just take it one day at a time. Just see how things go. I'd stay away from dope. Mostly I'd take it one day at a time.

I've been divorced for ten years and been living by myself. I've had a few relationships living with girls; lived with them six months, nine months, maybe a year here and there. And I had a didn't-give-a-shit attitude. I was working quite often making my own money. I quit drinking in 1980. I was smoking a lot of pot, doing a little bit of speed, and getting in with the wrong crowd, so to speak. You know, a straight john works nine to five. I was more of a – not a party type guy – but I liked to go out and do different things. Like if I wanted to drive from Edmonton to Vancouver one weekend or go for a week I could go. I didn't have anything holding me back. Now I'm at the stage where I've had a lot of time to think about it and it's time to settle down and take everything in a different perspective. You know, slow things down. You start to think about doing something before you do it. Whereas out there, I'd just do a lot of things without even thinking; just go out and do it, because it just happened to be there at the time and it was the thing to do, right? Now I take more time to think things through. I guess that's one good thing this place has done.

But I really don't have anything good to say about the place. You feel like cattle being herded into a stall every night when they lock you up. You know the way I pictured it when I tried to explain it to my ex-wife, about doing life 25, because for somebody out there it's kind of hard to comprehend what it must feel like. So I told her, I said, picture yourself falling into a tunnel, totally dark, and it's going to take you twenty-five years to walk out. It's totally dark in there; you don't know anything about what it's like in there and you have to take it one step at a time to get through this tunnel. I said, just try to imagine that. That's what it sort of feels like towards me, because when I came here, I didn't know a thing about nothing in here. Like I didn't know what to expect. It was total darkness to me. And I know it's going to take twenty-five years to get out and you have to take it one step at a time and you have to be careful every step you take, because you don't know what to expect. Just try to comprehend taking twenty-five years to go through that tunnel. I said that's sort of what it feels like to me. That's the best way I can explain it.

Imagination? Not much. There's nothing much here to use it on. Some nights you know you're sitting in the unit, you go and have a shower and a shave, and put a little cologne on, and kind of picture yourself, thinking, Jesus Christ, it would be nice to be heading out, going to a party, or going over to your girlfriend's, and getting all showered up. And then you get out of the shower and you're back in your cell. You know, from ecstasy to that same old depressing feeling. Like, fuck, it's never going to change. It's just over and over and over the same thing. I hate every second that I have to be here, every second. Yeah, there's a lot of times when you have this phoney smile on your face, but you're never happy about anything here. You know, when you lose your freedom, you've lost everything.

UPDATE

John petitioned for a new trial: it was granted and he was found not guilty and released. We were not able to contact him for a follow-up interview.

BARRY

'I'm just making progress as fast as I can, trying to consume the time.'

Barry was twenty-one when sentenced to life-25. He had served three years at the time of his interview.

Kent is the only prison I can actually say I've been in, unless you count Oakalla. Kent is so much cleaner than Oakalla. Oakalla you're hacking and choking all day long on dust. And I've only been here for a couple of years. I stay away from some of the programs due to the fact that I don't like some of the people that are in there. It's not that I don't like the person, I don't like the personality that goes with the person. I took a life skills course and I found it to be a joke. It does seem pointless, but it did teach me a few things. The little bit that it did is it taught me how to rationalize out my thoughts a little better than what I was doing before. Instead of jumping to a conclusion, right off the hop, I would sit down, debate the problem in my head, and then make appropriate actions. It's all right to think around here, but just don't do the actions, unless you're totally 100 percent sure of what you're doing. Because if there's the slightest chance of retaliation, let's say you irritate somebody the wrong way or something, you could get yourself into a problem. I've got so much on the go all the time, there's times I lose weeks where I don't realize that the way has gone by, I've done so much. I might start counting the days or years at some point, or whatever. I can't be bothered with that right now. I'm just making progress as fast as I can, trying to consume the time.

I came from a fairly strict household, you had to have permission before you went out. Your parents had to know the people you were associating with. It really helped when they knew the guidance counsellor at school, and he blackballs everybody that you associate with. I didn't apply myself due to the fact that people I could relate the best to were at the bottom of the barrel, as in marks-wise, attitude-wise, everything, so I just adjusted my attitude so that I could associate with that group.

I'm serving a life sentence for the murder of my mother. The factors surrounding this crime are inconsequential. At the time the crime took place, I was a very lonely and confused person who had few friends and even fewer people I could trust. Life for me was a downward spiral that seemed to have no bottom. Needless to say, I found the bottom, and found it without ceremony.

Looking back, I was always crying out to my family for help, but I could never verbalize what exactly I need help with.

I was terrified of my father. To him I was not the son he wanted. He desired a clone of the rest of the kids in the neighbourhood, the good "dutiful" sons. In me he got something completely different, I was unlike any of the other kids in the area. My father was a man who was well respected in the business community, but had little time for a family. He was constantly moving the family so that he could move on to bigger and better businesses. Very little consideration was given to the family.

My relationship with my mother was completely different. She always placed great expectations on me. I was going to be great, I was going to be better than everybody else. She only wanted me to be a success, anything short of that would be heartbreaking for her. We interacted, but how do you ask your mother to help you find a shrink because you are cracking up and having homicidal thoughts?

Out of sheer desperation, believing that there was no love in my family, I acted out my thoughts. When I was finished my mother was dead and two others [father and sister] were near death in the hospital.

I'm trapped in time. Sure, the time's going to go by. I'm losing fifteen to twenty-five years of my life, but I don't have to lose that time. I can actually use that time to be productive. I can get all sorts of things accomplished. On the street, I wouldn't have even considered going to school. A typical day … it varies from person to person – for me it's just getting up, and I get up in a good mood, which kind of irritates a few people around here. Because I don't care. I portray that I-don't-care attitude. I watch my step closely in the morning, because there's a lot of people that aren't so easygoing: so it takes them a few hours to get going in the morning. I have to be a little careful. But I'm in a good mood all the time. I can't look back, if I look at this with a sour attitude every day, I'm not going to go anywhere; but the day in general goes by fairly quickly for me, because I get myself involved first thing in the morning in what I'm doing. And if I don't get myself involved first thing in the morning, I go back to sleep. Every now and then I go through a couple or three days when I'm depressed. I should withdraw, but I don't – I get myself more involved. And it looks like it's never going to end.

I'm the sort of person, I don't like problems around me, because it takes away from my attention span, and I can't focus if I have to start watching my back all the time. I'm not going to be able to focus myself in on what I'm doing. It all depends on your roommate, too; if he's an understanding person, the two of you can get along on a social basis, and on a work basis. I've got a roommate that understands that when I sit down to work, I don't like interruptions. So, he leaves me alone, and I leave him alone. When I go to play the system I play it for one person and one person only, and that's me. If I can work a staff member to my advantage, I will. I'm straight upfront about it, too. I'll tell the guy straight out that I'm going to work him and that way he knows exactly where I'm coming from. There's all sorts of herring in the system that you can pull out and use to your advantage: it's just a matter of finding them, and if you don't work them deceitfully, you'll find that they're a whole lot easier to work. As long as the guy realizes you're sincere and honest about what you're doing, even though he knows he's getting worked, he's more susceptible. It depends on who's working. You've got these sickies who are in the office because there's a woman there. You find these guys that they can't control their sex urge – get themselves thrown in here, and the first thing is running after every skirt they see in the place. I was out there in GP very briefly. It was a political situation that I felt better that I leave the area while I was still alive, instead of going through all sorts of fights and this, that and the other thing, and having to watch my back twenty-four hours a day.

I'm looking at it this way: most of these guys that go yak about their date, this, that and the other thing, I'm so bad, I'm this, I'm that, I'm this, and I'm that – they're really institutionalized, they'll be back. It's like a big family, they're always coming back. They go out for a while, experience the street, and then come back scared: I couldn't make it so I fucked up again and came back to three square meals a day. I don't know what doing time does to a person – maybe it mellows them out a bit. Because I find that after this here, I've been more of a mellow person. I don't know what happened to me, or whatever, but all of a sudden I lost all the aggression that's in me. I'm actually more easy-going than I used to be. I used to jump at anybody. All you had to do was say boo to me, and I'd be, okay, well let's go … I got nothing to lose … all wounds heal. But now, I couldn't care less about it. A physical encounter now is nothing but a hassle for me. It's me. I made the conscious decision, it was in

Oakalla, after a guy got me going one day. I wound up doing ten days in the hole because I beat him up. And I sat there, and I go, what the hell did I do that for? He got my goat, he twisted it around and now I'm sitting here paying the price. I'm spending ten days here wondering, well, what am I supposed to be doing? It sounds like nothing for a sentence. In Oakalla, there are little itty-bitty quiet cells there, and you can't measure time in there because you've got no light. You can tell time by the time your meals come around, but it's almost like a dead pattern. You've got no freedom, you can't get up and flush your toilet whenever you want and you can't get a drink whenever you want.

I could call a few people my friends, but even though I associate with them here, I wouldn't associate with them on the street. I would say about one percent of the people I associate with in here, I would associate with on the street. I look back at it, how it didn't even faze me. I knew as the crime was committed I was going to jail. I had prepared myself mentally for it, so, anything less than a twenty-five-year sentence, I was going to take as a gift, like some-body's saying, well, it wasn't that bad, we're going to lessen your time. I had previous experiences with the court system, I'd watched it work before and you're basically at its mercy. Sure, it shook me right off the hook, but after the initial shake is finished, it's a lot eas-ier to live with because you don't look down the road. I just look into the immediate future: what I'm going to do in the next three months. With school, I've divided the year up into semesters, I don't worry about next semester until pretty close to the end of the next one, of this one. Like now I'll start planning for next semester, but it's just a matter of breaking the year into three bits. That way, you don't look at it as a full year, you're looking at it, without thinking about the time around me, without trying to take the jail into con-text. As I got to live here, I don't like to think about it all the time. I try to break away from the jail, they may have my body, but they're definitely not going to get my mind.

I figured, given my psychological reporting that I had done for the court case, I figured that they may just automatically try to put me into RPC. No. They said, well look, we'd like you to go, but there's no way we're going to take you there, too big of a headache. They're going to want me to do the violent offenders program; I can't see anything more. Sure, I'd like to do it right away … get it over with, get it out of the way. If you've got any sort of intelligence, you've automatically got a step on them and they're already intimidated by you. So, actually, the education thing works against me – it's counter-productive. I find the system that works the best with them is play innocent and play stupid. If you don't know what's going on around you, they figure they're in the driver's seat again. That's the only spot they want to be in, they don't want to be a passenger in somebody else's car. In order to do things you have to play the duck. Like the way I deal with these guys here – you've got to put the question to them, develop a certain answer, or lead towards an answer, and let them come up with it. So that way they feel a sense of accomplishment. I find it works great. I'm a realist, and I'm a materialistic person: if I can't feel it and I can't touch it, it's not there; if I can grab it and hold it, it's there and that's reality. You have your physical world and your perceptual world. Your physical world is: I'm here. My perceptual world is: I perceive the staff, as trying to do what they're doing – they're doing their job, and every now and then you get the odd one that wants to jerk you around, and this and that, and the only way I can perceive myself getting out of this physical world is by going through on what's getting me progress right now.

They don't let me see what the institution is writing on me right now. All I was shown when I asked for my stuff was the RCMP records. And the RCMP have got me painted as something violent and this, that, and the other thing. I found, they said, well, he's violent, he's this, he's that, he's manipulative. It's either going to be the situation where I do more time, or I don't. And I'm hoping and I'm working towards it, and I'm trying to work everything I'm doing into the point where I don't have to do more than the fifteen. Right now, I'm applying myself but I'm not running on all eight cylinders, like a car engine. Look at it this way, I'm sure I could score A's on all the tests and all that, but I see no purpose in that right now. It's like, I've read stories about guys who read so much, do so much where they overload their mind, and I'm not going to allow that to happen. I want to make sure everything's going well until I approach the fifteen-year judicial review, and then I can turn it on, and just start cranking the volume up on it all.

It's really irritating when the institution's psychologist, all he wants to do is write negative about you, because that's the easiest thing to write. He can't say positive, because positive screws the system. The system looks at positive: he's making progress — we don't like that. So this guy here, all he is is a character assassin. There was only one other spot they could have put me, that was into the nut-house. That means I would have to go in there, go through their program, and then let them decide when I was suitable to go back onto the street. I had a doctor, a psychiatrist, say to me: well, it would probably be about seven years before we would even consider letting you back out on the street; we see enough problems in you that we could keep ourselves busy, and basically what I was reading into what he was saying was, I'd make a great case study for him. No, the psychologists never saw me as violent. They saw multiple split personality or etcetera. I don't know where they even came up with that. It's kind of funny, but when they were interviewing me, I was scared. That's the best way to put it. I didn't know what the outcome was going to be. Yet I knew what the outcome was going to be. And the best thing I could do was bullshit the guy, in order so that I could try to work it to my advantage in court, so that there may enough questionable doubts that something could happen.

They say it costs $80,000 a year to keep us here. I'm going by the model and I'm not going to let them get away without spending that $80,000 a year on me. If they say that's what the norm is for a maximum-security inmate, I'm making sure I'm getting it. But for that $80,000 a year, I see three staff members sitting in the office playing chess all day, and that sort of bullshit. And they don't want to do nothing. They could take out one of those other people, or take it down to one person and, therefore, limit the staff – cut the staff back to a bare minimum. And then increase the programs, that would help. They say in maximum-security you're always under the gun. I sit here in the school and there is no gun in the school. I go into the unit and – the guy in the bubble, he don't care, he's half asleep all the time – guys are getting beat up in the shower in the hole all the time. I said, well, so what's the use, it's not maximum security, it's a joke! I'm a self-sufficient person. I do what I have to do in order to survive for myself – it's purely a self-preservation way of operating I work in. We've got guys who sit in the office there, and they do nothing. And it's purely frustrating when a guy asks, can you help me fill out a transfer? And he goes, well, I can't do that today, I got other things on the go – and you see him sit there and watch TV all fucking night. And he doesn't want to do nothing. The inability to do their job creates the tension. If everybody cooperated – cooperation here doesn't mean we've got to like one another, it just means we've got to work together on an understanding – we can actually get things accomplished. Most of the staff have got this attitude, we won't do fuck all for the convicts. And the convicts go, well, since he's got that attitude – fuck all pigs! That's another one, the mission statement. It is the guiding rules by which both people have to operate. But it's kind of unfortunate, they force you to operate by it, and yet you can't operate by it – or they don't operate by it. The minute you open up the book and you go, well, rule such-and-such here says you must do this, and he goes, the only thing that book's good for is wiping your ass. It means – it doesn't apply to him, but it applies to you.

I talk with my sister who's on the street, and she's talking about people that have the same personality traits as myself, that are troubled individuals. Doesn't mean they're going to commit murder, or whatever, but you need people that would give them a good shaking, explain the situation to them – like a youth counsellor, or something like that. Right at that time that it all happened, I went through a lot of emotional turmoil, where I just wasn't me for the longest time. I made a conscious effort to make sure I never walk around in a fog like I did. It went on for roughly about five years. I drank a lot, I drank like a fish all the time. I was bound and determined to get an ulcer. I said to myself mentally, I'm going to get an ulcer, so I go out and I drink and I drink and I drink and I drink. And it did nothing for me, all it did was waste all the money I had in my pocket. So, I'd walk into a bar with five hundred dollars, and decide, you're going to get drunk, I'm not going to leave until it's all gone. Now I'm looking at it this way: if I can get out of here, a normal person who's gone through his education and all that, a university degree, it's going to be … going to be like a normal person coming out of school. I've spent all my time in school.

It's just a matter of whether I'm going to let myself evolve finally or if I'm going to walk out and try to be a twenty-one-year-old again on the street. Some of these guys that come in at age, let's say, a guy comes in at age twenty and he acts like he's age twenty all the way through here. Then goes back on the street and pretends he's twenty again. Even though he's done ten years; he's now thirty years old. I'd say maybe about one percent are actually trying to better themselves. All the rest can't be bothered. The guys that aren't making progress are the guys that have got a definite release date. If I have a definite release date, I might have a totally different attitude. It's like the carrot in front of the mule. But I look at some other guys here that are trying to make a good go of it – they're trying to make as much progress as they possibly can – I can see that some of these guys aren't going to return. The majority? I had a guy say to me, well, I like this place. He goes, I'll go in and I'll tell the parole board, hey this place is great! I hope your taxes go up so my standard of living goes up.

UPDATE

When Barry was interviewed at RPC in the summer of 1994, the first thing he said was that he was "no longer a pompous, arrogant, obnoxious punk," as he had sounded to himself when he re-read his first interview. He added that he was "still conniving," but in a much more constructive manner. He had gone from Mission, where he had spent two years, to William Head on the condition that he would accept RPC when an opening came up. His session at RPC was almost over and was judged "one of the best experiences of my life" for it was "a chance to grow emotionally and intellectually." He had full family support and pointed out the special significance of this in his case since his crime had involved assaults on and the death of a family member. Some of the best staff at Mission had been like a father to him in terms of straightening out some of his views. He was glad that he hadn't gone "the Riverview route," which his lawyer had advised, even if it would have meant he'd have been out by now. Barry outlined the various components of the RPC program, drawing particular attention to the empathy and rational-emotive therapy sections and how they had helped him see himself and his problems, so that he had become a "more stable and balanced person." His sister had introduced him to a woman who had been his girlfriend for two years. He figured that he had grown nine or ten years in the last eight months and compared himself to "an old car that had been refurbished." He felt the problem with the life-25 sentence is that it "doesn't take into account growth" and that, as studies have shown, after the first seven years the experience of prison is counterproductive. "But prison is not a complete sewer if one knows how to actively pursue goals. It's been a growing experience that I wouldn't trade for anything. I still don't have a direction in life, but I know that I am slowly going to eventually find it – maybe I'm on the path and I don't even know it."

FRANK

'Now I must endure it, I must be better than normal.'

Frank was twenty when sentenced to life-25. He had served three years at the time of this interview.

The only federal prison I've been in is Kent Maximum. I've already completed three, I'm in my fourth year. I would say Oakalla is outdated. By comparing the two, Kent is a much more modern facility. There is more freedom of movement in Kent than there is in Oakalla. There's a lot more personal effects that you're allowed to keep. Your cell space is more your own – at the same time it's not because of double-bunking here, whereas in Oakalla it's single bunking.

The Oakalla jailbreak? What started it was an officer insulted an inmate in view of other inmates. At the time it started, it was the driving force to the riot that occurred December 28th of 1987. When the riot went down, there was a smash-up. A lot of porcelain was broken up; there was a lot of noise, a lot of water everywhere. The next day, after they brought the fire hoses around and everybody got wet, windows got broken and it was freezing cold. They came in, grabbed a bunch of us, took us to the cowbarn, which is an underground, subterranean, concrete crypt. You couldn't put your arms ... you could touch them wall to wall ... you couldn't stand up straight. There's water coming down the walls and then I heard some screaming and shouting on New Year's Day, just after midnight and it awoke me. I saw movement, I couldn't really tell what was what and who was who. I'd heard stories about the barn, so I figured it was some guard giving it to an inmate, they had the keys, but it turned out an inmate had gotten free from his cell, and had subdued the guard, got the keys and released everybody else. And the guy that released me, just looked at me and said, run! I went out to get my shoes. Somebody had already taken my shoes, so I left in stockinged feet, climbed the fence, and when I got to the top of the fence my feet slipped out and I cut my stomach open on the razor wire, so I was bleeding pretty badly − and then I ran down to the Deer Lake Park area, all through the bushes, and my feet got bruised up pretty bad. Eventually, I found a safe place to stay − I was with another inmate. And when I was apprehended, after about seventeen hours, it was at gunpoint, and I was very nervous that day.

I came in January of '87. I spent a month between then and January 1st of '88 in the Forensic Psychiatric, for trial evaluation. So, I'd say about ten months at Oakalla. Well, I work full time aside from coming to the Simon Fraser courses. I like to do a little creative writing on the side, and I draw quite frequently. I still find moments where I sit around and I feel vacant and bored. I don't know if it's hit me yet. Sometimes I sit back and I think about 2012 as my parole eligibility date. I think about it. It hurts inside, it's very painful, but it's not the end of my world. It's not going to rule my life − I'm not going to focus on that point. I still have options available to me; I'm not totally without hope.

I'd just turned twenty when I was convicted of first-degree and given life-25. As a juvenile I had a number of break and enter, and thefts under and over [$1000, with thefts over $1000 being "grand" theft]. Yes, I finished high school and I was seventeen when I graduated high school. I attended post-secondary education at a community college. I wasn't doing well; I hadn't really applied myself. I graduated high school easily. I never failed any classes, but I scraped by with the barest of minimums. I'd say my social life was to some degree somewhat retarded in some areas, while extremely active in other areas. I played rugby. I was engaged in a lot of extra-curricular activity in high school. I hung out a lot with my friends. I hadn't really gotten into the drugs at that time. One sister, one brother, both younger. My mother, who is divorced, she has a new man in her life. My father's been up to see me once, but he's got to come from the Prairies. My girlfriend came to see me prior to my conviction, and asked me whether or not I would marry her. She asked me if I would marry her – after I'd been charged. I told her I had to wait until the trial was finished with before I made any decisions. And once I was convicted, I told her that it would probably be in her best interests if she found somebody else. My feeling for her is that I felt so much for her, I didn't want to confine her. It's … it's hard to say. I mean, there's such an intense feeling, not only when we are able to be physical with one another, but on an emotional level. There was a void, a hollowness, that she fills in me, and something I do for her.

When I was first charged, I'd come to the point – I was in Oakalla at the time – I had decided that I would kill myself. At that time I had made in my mind the decision that I didn't feel I had the right to live. From that day, I was looking for some way to do it. I was looking for a blade, I was looking for a piece of rope – anything to end my life. Because I felt so miserable. I was on a, I guess, a self-pity trip. Like, that's all I can say it was. Often at night I lay in my bunk and I think about that. And sometimes I think that my being recaptured was a blessing in disguise. Because, I think, had I remained out, I would have hurt some people, and that would have destroyed me inside – emotionally, physically, anyway – to stay out.

At a party, with some mutual friends, I met one of the individuals with whom I was involved in the incident. The other individual I'd known for some years, we played a fantasy role-playing game together. And an individual approached me and addressed the issue of murder of certain people. These people were very close to the individual. Looking at the relationship I share with my counterparts, I took it lightly. I didn't believe it, I didn't feel that his intentions were indeed to do this. This individual at that time was very insecure, very in need of a dominating force in his life. I used forms of manipulation to control this individual. I was getting into drugs at the time. I was in a limbo, I was kind of lost, I didn't know what I would do with my life. So, I used this individual to acquire money to buy drugs, to pay for gasoline for my vehicles. And when he proposed the deal, I went along with it too. Placate him, so I could continue the role I had been using. And it went so far as to be at the house when it transpired, though I was not in the room. Well, I had been told that it would happen. I, I ... because of the relationship I share, the strength of the relationship, the bond that I had with the counterparts, my parents, I couldn't believe that someone else would feel differently. So, when it happened, when murder started, I heard it in my head, I heard all the screams, I heard the hits, I could hear the sounds ... and I tried to run. I just wanted to get out, and I couldn't move. It's like the dream where you're standing on a railway track. And, you can hear the train behind you, you can't see it, but you can hear it, you know it's there, but you can't move. Everything is slow motion. That's what it was like for me that night. I stood in the hallway outside the bedroom door, and then one of the individuals came to me with the bludgeon which was a baseball bat that he had used. There was blood running down it. He held it in front of me and he said, it's your turn. I was supposed to beat a fifteen-year-old girl to death. I said, no, I can't, I'm not a killer. I can't kill. The mother died. The father was attacked – both his arms were broken, his eye was out, most of his teeth were removed, he had a fractured skull. I think it was one of the individual's cries against what had happened to him during his childhood.

I would like – if I had my way – if I could do what I truly wanted to do, I would devote myself right now thoroughly to education; obtain some type of advantage, something I can use, because I know when I get back to the street, this stigma of prison will always be there. Until I die. So, I'll need some type of advantage. Something that will set me apart from everybody else, so I can walk in if I need a job, and I have this; and I can lay the papers down and say: I've got this, I've worked hard. My appeal comes up in June. I'm not going to try to snow you here, I'm obviously not totally 100 percent innocent of what transpired. After the incident took place, I assisted in the removal of certain articles that were obtained from the house. I don't know whether I did so out of fear or what was the motivation behind it, but I was involved. With the appeal, I hope that I can say what I didn't have a chance to say at the trial. I will take the stand in the appeal; I will try to portray the events as they transpired to me. I will say these things and let the jury decide, and hopefully they will see that, though I was there, I'm not guilty of first-degree murder. I expect it will go quite well. I have a little bit of trouble dealing with the authoritarian figures here, but, smart enough to realize that I have to play the game if I want to get by. So, I've been doing it.

When I first came to Kent, because of the nature of the trial – the high profile – there was a lot of tension. And when I came to Kent, I first came to B Unit, and I know a lot of people still out here in population and they're still my friends. Some people felt that somehow I could be a threat or something, they felt they didn't want me there. Now at the time, I had a marriage coming up, I had an appeal in the works. I have never taken human life but, if I had stayed out there, either my life would have forfeit, or I would have killed somebody else. And I didn't want to resort to that. So, you may say it was a coward's option – I'm not happy about being in protective custody – but I'm happier here than in general population. It was my decision to come this way, contrary to the belief that all protective custody inmates are skinners or rats. Before coming to protective custody, that was my consensus. That's what you learn in population – that they are there, this is why they're there. Since having come here, I've made quite a few friends here. I'm not worried about somebody coming up behind me; I'm not walking around with *Playboy* shoved in the back of my pants, or worried about someone trying to shank me in the spine. There was a stabbing here last week! So, I mean, they happen all the time.

A lot of people here blame the external world for their troubles: they're not big enough to accept the fact that they are responsible for their own situations. There's guys here that I can deal with on a one-to-one basis, guys that understand what I'm going through, guys that you can talk to, eh. And oh, there's people you can associate with and people you can't associate with, people you can trust, people you can't trust. There's no carrot for lifers. They can't dangle anything in front of your face. I mean, the only thing they have is the Special Handling Unit. It comes back; one of the things that I first heard when I came to prison, before I was convicted, was that if I was convicted, the second one's free. That's what they say. I could kill somebody now, and I wouldn't get any more time. Because they cannot add to the twenty-five years. What they say is: you're eligible for parole after serving twenty-five. That's just eligibile, there's no guarantee that if you go through all the hoops … I could wind up spending the rest of my life in prison. Regardless of what I do. Whether I play the game, whether I deal with these people, whether I go through all the programs. I attempt to help myself but they may just decide in the end that I'm too dangerous to be released back into society. There's no guarantee that I'll ever see the street again … none. So, that's what they're saying, that's why they're so dangerous. With life-10, if there's a subsequent incident, they can be moved to life-25. There's that hanging hoop. People doing straight ten years they do six and they're on mandatory.

When I heard the verdict, I looked at my mother. My mother was standing behind the accused box. My mother was holding her hands to her face; my grandmother was beside her, and I felt like crying. I felt like laughing ... I felt like ... just fainting. All these emotions were just flooding through me. My mother was just shaking her head. I told her prior, don't cry. If I'm found guilty, don't cry – 'cause I wouldn't have been able to help it, I would have cried. Instead, I turned to the judge, and ... I just smiled. I chuckled a little bit. I bent down and talked to my lawyer, and asked him if I could say something to the judge. And he asked me if it was going to be sarcastic. I said, of course. And he said, no, because we have an appeal coming up. And when I was exiting the courtroom, I struck the wall, the back wall of the courtroom, which was hollow, the stairway led up behind it, and the whole wall reverberated – there was a tremendous boom. I think that showed how I felt. I felt angry, I felt mad, I felt sad, and I felt really bad. Riding back to the pre-trial centre, both my co-accused were crying, and I tried to comfort them as best I could. They seemed to lose their strength, and by their weakness, I gained strength, and I tried to help them. I went to Oakalla; I escaped; I was returned to Oakalla. I was deemed too dangerous to hold in Oakalla, so I was moved to Vancouver pre-trial centre, to Kent, and then from Kent back to pre-trial for the escape charge, and then back from pre-trial to Kent. When I came to Kent, to B-Unit, I checked into pop. Just a few days ... a feeling out period. And, then I came to protective custody, and when I returned to pre-trial, I returned to population pre-trial. Because I knew everybody that was there, and I had no problems with these people. Then when I returned here, I returned to protective custody.

I think the institution sees me as a controlled individual. I rarely have been involved in incidents, demonstrations against the administration. I haven't had an institutional charge. I've received excellent reports. A progress summary that one of the Living Unit officers did on me, it was extraordinarily favourable, and I think I'm perceived in a fairly decent light. My lawyer was trying for a criminal negligence charge, which is third-degree murder – manslaughter. Which would have been acceptable, because I knew I had the information in my head that it was going to happen … and I did nothing to stop it. I was there, I was ten feet away.

Everybody has some little thing … everybody has some little thing that helps them get through the day; some thought that bounces back and forth across their head, something that offers them hope, some chance to prove yourself. These people that are advanced in their sentences, I would say they've handled it, they've managed to deal with the time they have. What they do with their time is up to them, it's in their hands. How they handle their time is in their hands, and if they're that far along, they've managed to cope with what they've had. It would depend on the individual. The term here, the real derogatory term used is goof. Someone calls you a goof, and that's a dying word. Some of these people who are doing life-25 are goofs. So, you don't deal with them.

My room-mate just came back in from mandatory supervision … so, I found myself dealing with all sorts of people – people who have months to go, people who have years. It's difficult. I find myself being a little resentful that they're getting out. Especially some of these people that go around bragging about the type of crime they're going to pull next. Because I know, in my heart, if I were to be legally set free, I would do my best to resurrect my life, to spend the time with my wife, to have children, and these people, all they can talk about is getting back out, shooting drugs in their arms. That bothers me, and some people, I'm genuinely glad they're going out because they're going to make an attempt to make something of themselves. But, like I said, there's the people that all they talk about are scores and drugs, and deep down I don't know if there's a cure, or a sure-fire answer for these people. I mean, some of these people are habitual criminals. I mean, that's what they exist for, some of them truly enjoy inflicting their will upon others, whether that's at the end of a gun, or whatnot. I don't know if you can find a cure, some way that you could train these people to adapt to society without becoming clones or automatons.

Double-bunking creates a lot of tension because you don't have any privacy. The only privacy you have is when you put the curtain up, your door's covered, the window's covered, and nobody can see in. That's the only privacy you have. And even then you have guards coming by on the hour pulling the curtain back. So, that's difficult. I would change it, I would single-bunk it. The greatest change I would put in is I would make sure they play the reward system here: if you're good, you get a reward. I would make these rewards based on individual merit. You earn it if you've earned it, and you've proven that you can be trustworthy – that's what I would change. These people could be reintegrated with society. Early transfers, even day-parole programs, where people are slowly reintegrated with society. And they can still be monitored to see how they deal with society, because every day, every minute we spend here, society changes. And I mean, along with the physical changes, there's moral, there's mental changes that occur within society. Without having the opportunity to reintegrate, you're going to have people who find themselves outcast, frustrated.

I don't know if I'm just being bitter, but I don't see how life-25 serves the individual or the state. It's obviously punishment. It's not an attempt to rehabilitate a deviant gone wrong – it's punishment. I've heard the Swedish system in particular deals with murderers in a different fashion. There's an attempt to rehabilitate, to understand, to learn, to change thinking that had gone wrong. With that, they're dealing with the problem – that's the problem. They're dealing with it. Here, they're putting the problem away – they're not dealing with the problem; they're shuffling it onto the back shelf, letting the dust accumulate until the day comes they've got to look at what they've got there, and this person might get out. People talk about institutionalization. You have to become institutionalized; no person can come through here, even during a year, without suffering some form of institutionalization. They speak, I move. That's the way it is. You can be rebellious and you'll just pay for it in the long run. Why be stupid? Why make your time harder? If following a simple directive will get you easier time, then do it. I find a lot of the guys doing the time I'm doing. Don't want to make waves; they just want to do their time. They're having trouble enough coping with it, dealing with it, handling it, that they don't need the extra baggage of … the word is "upstart punk." These ones that are always in the face of the guards – all it does is make them ornery, and it just makes everybody suffer.

Some of the staff are all right. I mean, they're good people, they make a genuine attempt to assist. They don't go out of their way to make trouble for you. You treat them like humans, they treat you like humans. And it's well appreciated, though you can't say it. Some take a delight in knowing that they have control over other people, and it's obvious, and all you can do is accept it. If you try to bug them, they'll use their authority to make you pay. To me there's no point in making it tougher – it's tough enough already. I have enough problems, enough things running through my head. I don't need to be worried about some officer doing something to make my hand more difficult.

I thought I'd be excommunicated from my family in a sense, but the support has been unreal. It's the the only thing that's kept me alive. Like I say, it was when I contemplated suicide – my father came in that day, that same day, for a visit and he wisened me up. He said: you can do it, I can't stop you … but just think about all the people you're leaving behind, think about the love there. That really hit home. That was the worst guilt trip I've ever been on, and since then suicide isn't an option. If my sentence is not altered in any way by the appeal, I would like to write a book. Not about the incident. I'd like to let that be in the past. I'd like to bury that and get on with my life ... even if I'm forced to live here. So, I'd like to write a book, it'd be very escape-fantasy-oriented because that's what occupies my mind, that's what helps me deal with my time. I ... have a very creative imagination, and sometimes I just close my eyes and allow myself to imagine and I'd like to transfer some of these onto paper. If I do get out in 2012, if it is then when I get out, I'd like to look at it as an adventure, a relearning process. I enjoy learning, I enjoy fragments of thought that I can use, that make me better. And, by going out there and seeing all these new things, I believe I'd initially be intimidated by it – to say I wasn't would be to lie – but I'd like to treat it like some type of adventure, relearning ... everything would have changed. You know I may be forty-five years old, body-wise, but my mind hopefully will forever remain young. My wife and I discussed the prospects of children, and at this time, prior to the appeal, we've decided to wait to see what the future holds. If the future holds a lesser sentence for me, a sentence with light at the end of the tunnel, prior to my being released, we'll try for a child, but, currently, we've talked it over ... she'd very much like to have a child ... I would not, because of the fact, by the time I got out now ... I'm twenty-three now, and turn twenty-four this year ... by the time I got out, my children would be twenty years old. They wouldn't know me – they'd come in on a visit and once, twice, three times a week they'd see a stranger in a chair, who they'd call Daddy and, it would ... it would hurt too much. There's only so much you can do. There's only so much you can learn. As I said society changes every minute. It's very stagnant, static here. My mind is still at twenty ... still. And as I said, my body may be older, but my mind hopefully will remain young. I think I'll be a twenty-seven-year-old man in a thirty-five-year-old's body when I come up for the judicial review. Because, I will change inside, dealing with my wife when she comes in, being married is a responsibility. I try to assist her where I can, where I'm able, but still, it's a part of me that's growing up, learning, adapting, but only to a small degree. It's like receiving information from society, but it's very filtered. I'd be about twenty-seven ... that's the point I will have reached by the time my body's at thirty-five. I think that, with her coming in, receiving that, using what I learn here, whether it's through courses I take at Simon Fraser, or from newspaper clippings I read ... everything is collected, but you can only grow so much without a practicum. I mean ... practicum ... it's ... I'm not sure of the word practicum – it's when you go out and do it, right?

I would like to see the twenty-five-year sentence reduced but, more than that, I would like to see it have meaning. To find out what's wrong ... what really transpired to make these events occur, and an attempt at rehabilitation for the wrong. That is what I would like to see. If that can be accomplished, I am sure restructuring the twenty-five-year sentence would follow. RPC approached me, but until my appeal is dealt with, they won't touch me. They would want me to take their violent offenders program. I've talked with a number of individuals that have been to RPC, and from what I've heard, it sounds almost like a reprogramming station. Reprogramming so that you will think this way, you will act this way, program responses to stimuli and it's like when the guy got the Nobel Prize for doing the lobotomies, he was eventually shot by one of his patients. I mean, it's still there! You can bury it, but you can't hide it. If you expose it for what it is, what's there, what's lurking deep in the individual's mind, if you can find that factor, identify it, and rectify it, that would be a big step. Somewhere along the line we were socialized – something happened that ... this kind of incident could occur. I used to think that because this happened, there was something wrong with me, and I'm not trying to blame it all on circumstance, or poor judgment, but now I would say that there isn't something wrong with me ... there's a part of me will forever remain dead after what happened. That can never be brought back to life, and that part was perhaps the part that went along with what transpired. I think that was where my problem was. Some people could probably look at me, and see a host of problems. Personally, I feel all right with myself right now. I can deal with myself; I can look at myself in the mirror, and say: that's okay. I can deal with that, whereas when I first came in it took me the longest time to do that, to realize that there wasn't some deep-rooted psychological problem. I don't now believe that I'm psychopathic, or sociopathic. I was at the wrong place at the wrong time, and that is why I am here now. But being at that place was by my choice, knowing or having the knowledge that what was going to happen happened, but not believing it – that was my mistake. Had I believed, I don't know what I would have done. We can all look back and use hindsight, and say if this, if that … I mean, we can change the world that way. But I have to look to the future now; I have to make myself better, I have to make myself presentable, because now I will be under direct scrutiny whereas there's millions of people out there that are perhaps far worse off – psychologically, emotionally, intellectually – than I am, that will never endure this scrutiny. Now, I must endure it, I must be better than normal.

UPDATE

In an interview at Mission Institution, summer of 1994, Frank said that he was still in "good spirits", that he had a more or less "free hand" working on his writing and that he had enjoyed the move from maximum-security Kent to medium-security Mission, which had taken place in 1992. His appeal had failed and "not a lot of hope was put into it." The RPC program was pending at this time and his wife was expecting a child. Strong family support continued, which made it possible for him "to go on." And he drew an analogy between his writing, which dealt with quest adventures, and his own situation, which he saw as "one of the greatest adventures" of his life: "to make himself better than normal." This was the "greatest adventure" and challenge since things were changing out there and there was a "gap" or "lost time": time moved differently inside as you were aware that you were not part of the progression out there. As for inside time, he said that at some point you have "to start setting the table to get out", to start thinking about the fifteen-year judicial review. He hoped to get his degree in psychology before his release, so he could get a job in education and "help children not come into a place like this."

'You're sentenced to life but they won't let you die.'

Al was thirty-one years old when he was sentenced to life-25. He had served five years at the time of the interview.

It's hard to describe a typical day, you get up, go for breakfast, come to work, go through the motions more than anything else. I'm fortunate I think in that I've got a job that actually has some responsibility inside the prison, which is really exceptional. And it also takes some time and occupies time to help it pass. But after the work day is over, if you're not into playing floor hockey in the gym, or lifting weights, then it leaves little else. The library is only open for an hour, and it's watch TV or play bridge in the unit.

Can I describe how I expect my sentence to proceed? No, I can describe how it's supposed to work, and the way it's supposed to work is that, through displaying what CSC considers appropriate behaviour, I should earn reduced security. And, based on their programs and their goals, and all this type of stuff, I should already be in a medium, but because I'm political within the institution, I think it will be a long time before I ever see one. I applied for a medium, but I think it'll be a long time before I ever see one. As far as the sentencing and parole, anybody serving a life sentence with a parole eligibility date of more than fifteen years is allowed to apply to the court that sentenced them – what they call the Court of Competent Jurisdiction – for a judicial review after fifteen years. And in this review, you can be awarded a reduced parole eligibility date; you can be told you're getting nothing, or you can be told to come back again in *x* number of years. Assuming you win judicial review, you then become parole-eligible. That doesn't mean you're going to get parole, you're just now eligible to apply to the National Parole Board. And they'll set up a pass program, whatever all else, at that time, but as far as looking forward to it, it's ten years down the road before I can even go through the judicial review, so I don't even think about it, it's a day at a time.

There's been three go before judicial review, and all of them have been some of the more heinous murderers in Canada – cop killers, and that type of thing, and they don't seem to be getting much. They're awarded reduced security, and to start on fast programs and this type of thing, but it's going to take a few more years for any real pattern to develop. I wish them luck. I sincerely do. I don't believe in the prison system the way it is now, because if there's any real rehabilitation, it's in spite of the system, not because of it. And most of the guys going out are going to reoffend. It's a sad fact, but it's true; they're going to re-offend in one way or another or they'll be back on a suspension because a possibility exists that they're going to reoffend. But I wish them luck, I like to see anybody get out. There are guys, career criminals, that'll tell you: I'm serving five years, or I'm serving ten years, or whatever, and when I get out I'm going to rob banks. That's all they know, that's all they're interested in. And there's nothing the system will ever do to change that. A person has to want to change.

I was thirty-one years old, didn't quite know what to expect … you've seen all the TV movies, and the hype and everything else and prison is nothing like the hype. But one of the attitudes that I had was that, first of all, I was not going to get political. And I did. The prison system works on its own set of rules called the Commissioner's Directives in the Penitentiary Service Regulations and if you buck the system, if you say that the CD is wrong, or if you even say the administration isn't living up to this policy or that policy, you're considered political. And, if you're going to be political, then you had better be actively political, in that you're elected to a position because those that are elected to positions are protected a little bit from the backlash of the administration. And those that are not elected to positions will find themselves on an airplane and waking up in a French-speaking prison in the morning.

I got political first of all in Edmonton over the education system — or lack of education system I guess is a better way to describe it — to a point where it cost me a transfer to Kent, which was all to my betterment because I'd been trying to get to Kent anyway, and they'd turned me down on three different occasions. But once I spoke out publicly, and it was broadcast on the news, against the education system in Edmonton, I was on an airplane to Kent very quickly. Education is the only really positive thing within prison. Once you've got it, they can't take it away from you. It doesn't matter what else there is. If you buy a TV, they can take it away from you, they can say you can't have that in your cell. If you do hobby work, they can take that away from you. They can take away the right to do hobby work. Once you've educated yourself, at whatever level, whether you've achieved Grade 6, Grade 8, or a university degree, that's a thing you've got and it's in you — they can't take it away. I'm active with the lifers group. I'm also the Inmate Committee rep for my living unit. Elected positions. I won't sit back and watch injustices against fellow prisoners. Many of them are under-educated and not capable of speaking out for themselves except in a violent tone, because that's what they've known all their lives. And I can handle it reasonably and rationally, so I'll speak out for them, and it causes strife. I'm doing more time in a max than I should because of it, but so be it. Over the last month, there seems to have been some movement on the part of this administration towards actually following the mission statement, and to finding out where their shortfalls are, and following the mission statement, and adjusting to it. And, I think it's because of pressures that have been brought to bear over the previous nine months, from April of last year, when the mission statement came out. Inmates are actually starting to use the mission statement, when they're filing grievances. Because up until a month ago, and I've said it in writing to the administration of Kent, that I firmly believe that the administration of Kent takes the mission statement as a public relations document that was issued by the Commissioner to appease the politicians and the public, and they have no intention of putting it into policy. It will, I think, in a few years have an impact, but it's going to take years.

It's a tough sentence. I mean, how do you describe it? It's the rest of your life. You're sentenced to prison not for ten years, or twenty-five years as people tend to believe; you're sentenced to prison for life. The sentence is life imprisonment with no eligibility for parole for at least twenty-five years. That doesn't mean you're getting out in twenty-five. That means you can apply. And nobody can fathom it. Nobody has served it yet, because it's only been in place since 1976. As I said, nobody can fathom it, nobody can really imagine what it's like to do it and everybody has to do it differently, because each person is an individual and has his own personality. I tend to say one day at a time. One day at a time … get up in the morning and see what the day brings. And, when the day is over, well that's past, there's no sense dwelling on it. Let's get up tomorrow and do one day again.

If you want to get into simple mathematics, shortly after you come into the system, you get a letter from the parole board and – this is really nice of them – you're sentenced to life-25, and you get a letter from the parole board that says, your parole-eligibility date is, in my case, April 13, 2010; however, you may apply for day parole on April 13, 2007! Really magnanimous of them. And they tell you, you must serve 9,131 days. Yes, they tell you exactly – you must serve 9,131 days … they've got it all counted out for you, including leap years, and it's just appalling. You can't afford to sit here and dwell on the fact that you've got twenty years to go, or twenty-one, or nineteen, or however close you happen to be getting, you can't dwell on that because it's unmanageable. I think if lifers started to dwell on the fact that they've got twenty years to go, or nineteen years to go, the suicide rate would be so high that they might as well bring back the death penalty. The difference between this death penalty and the death penalty they had before was they got it over with quick; now they make you suffer. They even have a neat little deal in the Commissioner's Directives where, if you're unhealthy, to the point where it is life-threatening, you can't refuse medical attention! They can stick you in a hospital and keep you alive, so you have to continue to serve your sentence. You're sentenced to life, but they won't let you die.

How can you describe the different types of guys? There's guys like myself that have never had a conflict with the law in their life, there are career criminals who've gone out and robbed banks, and in some cases that's all they've done is rob banks. There are others that shot somebody in the course of a robbery and therefore are serving life for that, there are drug dealers, there are drug dealers that have killed people in drug deals and are serving life for that. It's as varied as anywhere else. The best way to describe a prison population, I guess, is a microcosm of the general population of this country. Except that it's single sex. I don't worry about who I'm living with. They all realize that I'm in here doing life-25 because I killed somebody, not because I walked into a drug store and grabbed a bag of whatever. Or grabbed a bank teller's cash drawer or something like that. It's because somebody pissed me off and they're dead. And the guys around me know that. And it's the same with every other lifer. The guys around them realize also that they're in here because they killed somebody. There's a degree of respect you know. This is this man's space. Within that, there's also the guidelines within the prison, and I'm not talking now about administrative rules, these are prisoners' rules. You've got the rules, you live within them and you stay within them. And as long as you're within those rules, really nobody's going to bother you. Right now there are fifty-some lifers in general population. And that includes, I should be careful to say, a couple of guys that aren't actually sentenced to life: there's one that's sentenced to forty-one years, another one to thirty-eight years. The sentence for first-degree murder as dictated by law is automatically life-25 – life imprisonment with no eligibility for parole for twenty-five years. The sentence for second-degree murder is life imprisonment with no eligibility for parole for at least ten years, or more as seen fit by the sentencing judge. The sentencing judge can give somebody life-10, life-12, or life-15 … that type of thing, on a second-degree charge, where on a first-degree charge it's automatically life-25. No life sentence can exceed the life-25.

The reports that are written by institutional staff are unimportant. They're written by semi-professional people that are taught how to write reports, not necessarily how to evaluate people, that sit there, thinking that because they've taken a case management course they're now psychologists and have the answers to all your problems. And I have a great deal of trouble with them. CSC thrives on paperwork, like any other bureaucracy, and what's written determines whether you go down in security, whether you get a proper parole board, all that kind of stuff. But to me it's unimportant. I know who I am, I can respect the person I see in the mirror in the morning, and I really don't care what they write. Everybody gets the opportunity to read and sign them; a lot of guys will just stuff them back in front of their case management officer. I haven't had a case management report done on me since August of '88. They're supposed to be done every four months, but the staff's afraid to write about me, because they know I'll challenge any lies they put in there.

Most of the jobs in here are meaningless. There are some jobs that aren't: the guys working the grill in the kitchen are learning a good skill. Working in the cabinet shop, they can learn a good skill if they put themselves to it, but most of the other jobs are delivering the toilet paper to the living-units – pretty important task, well it is, everyone's got to have toilet-paper, right – but, you know, it's not exactly what you would call a job. A kitchen job is pulling the meal wagons down to the closed units – that's a job, all you do is pull this wagon through the courtyard three times a day. That's your total work day. Pretty tough job, pretty meaningful stuff. I can see a person getting a lot out of that, knowing how to pull a wagon across the city of Vancouver, or whatever. You know, maybe they'll be able to deliver papers, or something significant when they can get out, because that's all that job is going to lead to.

The Commissioner's Directives suggest that "there be a meaningful work placement." This is the term they use for every prisoner in the institution. And I've already described what's meaningful – delivering toilet paper, the janitor that sweeps the floors. That's all meaningful employment as far as the institution is concerned. There is supposed to be work placement available, full-time placement for every prisoner in the institution. There's not. I don't know what can be done about it, if anything. It's just the structure of the prison that says, it is or isn't going to work, and there just isn't that much work. I don't know what can be done. By the time you've been in long enough to be going through your appeals and everything else, and that's when you finally realize that, yes, I'm going to serve this sentence, you've found a full-time job. And usually one that you're comfortable with. A lot of the guys aren't interested in meaningful work, they're interested in picking up enough inmate pay to keep themselves in tobacco and cans of Coke or coffee, whatever it is they're interested in, never mind the rest.

The jury came back with a guilty of first-degree murder, the judge had no choice in what sentence he handed down – it's automatic, life-25. The judge had the opportunity, and in my case should have availed himself of that opportunity, to take the first-degree away from the jury so they couldn't consider it. Even though you're charged with first-degree, if the prosecution hasn't proven the case, they've still proven that, yes, the murder did take place – but they haven't proven both planned and deliberate, which is what's required. Not planned *or* deliberate, planned *and* deliberate. And, if the prosecution hasn't proven that, the judge has the right to take first-degree away from the jury so they can't consider it; they can still come back with a verdict of second-degree or manslaughter. In my opinion, I'm guilty of manslaughter; probably, in the eyes of the law, I'm guilty of second-degree. If I'd been found guilty of second-degree, I would have been sentenced to life-10. On life-10, you're eligible for day parole in seven years. I've served five. If I'd got life-10, I'd be eligible for day parole in two more years; because I got life-25, I'm eligible for day parole in seventeen more years.

In my opinion, the sentence should be life-7, not life-25. It doesn't matter whether it's first-degree, second-degree, or manslaughter – even manslaughter should be life-7. And the person should serve the full seven years – no day parole in four, five, and six, they should serve the full seven years. And after that seven years, as long as institutional behaviour has been deemed acceptable, they should be granted parole. And on that parole, allowed to go back out and rebuild their lives in the community, and do whatever … and if they screw up, none of this bring them back for a year and kick them out again. Bring them back. They're sentenced to life – bring them back. But give them a chance. This will be similar to Sweden's system and, as I say, if they screw up there's no need for trials, there's no need for anything, because it's a parole violation. It doesn't cost the government a fortune in trials – you just put them back in prison and they stay in there forever.

The life-25 will probably be reconsidered; not out of compassionate grounds, but out of economic necessity. And if it's reconsidered, I would expect that what you would see is something like life-15. If judicial reviews are proven to provide an advantage to the majority of life-25ers, that will trigger a justification to the politicians to reduce it to life-15 because those that wouldn't win a judicial review also wouldn't win parole; therefore, they don't have to let them out at the fifteen, and they can reduce their costs. Any such changes won't affect me. About the time the decisions to change come will be about the time that I'm parole-eligible anyway.

I'm fully aware of the fact that I don't require maximum-security handling – my work supervisor will tell you I don't require maximum-security handling, and you know yourself from dealing with me that I don't. On the other hand, I can go through this prison and show you many that do. So, I can't say eliminate maximum-security prisons. They certainly need a better method of assessment, a fairer method of determining who does and doesn't get transfers, so the decisions aren't personal. I've taken some political action, filed a grievance against this staff member or that staff member, or whatever, and won that grievance, and now that staff member is making a decision on whether or not I move down in security. It's now become a personal decision, instead of one that should be made rationally and objectively. I don't know how to eliminate that, but there has to be steps to eliminate it.

For me the question is in the end only academic. I believe I'm going to die in prison. Maybe in 1990, maybe in the year 2000, maybe in the year 2010. The environment is such that I am living with, and considered one of Canada's either most dangerous or most unmanageable prisoners. That's why I'm in a max. That is what a max is supposed to be for: Canada's most dangerous or most unmanageable prisoners. Based on that fact – and I live in a population of 140 or 150 of Canada's most undesirable people – there's a good chance that somebody for some foolish reason could decide they're taking me out. They're drunk on brew, they're pilled up, I've done something that they didn't like. And the same holds true for me. I'm not likely to, but I could. I honestly believe I'll die in prison. Because I'm a fatalist. When my time is here, it's here, and there's nothing I can do about it. You can't speed it up, you can't slow it down.

I think I have definitely matured, if that's the right word, and I'm not even sure that that is. I think things through a lot more, a lot deeper, than I ever did on the street. On the street, it was just, sort of, oh well if you screw it up you can fix it tomorrow. Well, in here, you screw it up, and you may not see tomorrow, you know! So, yeah, you think things through a lot more closely. People in here, most of them, manage to function at the mental age that they should have been at and weren't at when they came in here. They should have been developing functionally as eighteen, nineteen, and twenty-year-olds, and weren't. Now they are. They won't go beyond that, they'll serve twenty-five years and come out as a twenty-year-old. Because they've missed the things that I did from twenty to thirty years of age, and the things that you did from twenty to thirty years of age, they've never had the opportunity to do, and without doing it you can't mature past it. The things that you did from thirty to forty years of age I've never had the opportunity to do, because I came to jail at thirty-one. When I get out, I'll behave like a thirty-one-year-old. Lifers don't reoffend when they're paroled. That's the typical, and I think it's like, point-nine percent have reoffended, or something like that, less than one percent. That doesn't mean they don't have the problems and other struggles, if you try to reintegrate with the friends you had before you came in. They've lived those twenty-five years, they've got twenty-five years of life experience that you don't have, and you can't conceive of what they're talking about because of it, so you have to go back to associating with younger people that haven't had that life experience, because it's the only way you can survive. And they do the same thing with prisoners when they get out of jail … we go out at, at fifty-six, when I'm parole-eligible, and I start running around with twenty-nine and thirty-year-old people, they're going to say, like, there's something psychologically wrong with this man.

If I come out at fifty-six, as a thirty-one-year-old, after twenty-five years in prison, I'll be the same mental age as my children. How do you deal with that? Assuming that I make it through this sentence, if I'm fortunate enough to, and I pray that I am, I don't want to die any more than any other person, I like living just as much as anybody else and if I make it through, I still wouldn't see my children. I would make a point of not seeing them. It's far better for them to have me not interfere with their life in any way, shape, or form.

What will I do then? Oh, I'm going fishing. If I get out, I'm going back to Northern Manitoba where I grew up; I'm going to build a little cabin on the side of the lake, and I'm going fishing. I'll go into town and get supplies, and say hi to people, and report to the parole officer and whatever, and go fishing. To hell with the world. I'm dropping out of society; I have absolutely no respect left for the Canadian government whatsoever. One of the things I did was three years in the army – I loved my country, believe it or not, very much. I loved my country. Definitely didn't agree with the politics, but when I was out there, I had the right to vote, the right to change things within the framework of the law. After having gone through what they call the justice system, which is inappropriately named – it's something like military intelligence, neither of them exist, the words don't fit together – and what I've seen within this prison, I have absolutely no respect left for this country whatsoever. I don't want anything to do with it. I'll do whatever time they tell me I have to do until I'm eligible for parole. Once I'm out, goodbye. I don't want to see them again, I don't want anything to do with them.

There's nothing to be gained except retribution for the life I took. There's no rehabilitation whatsoever. If there is any rehabilitation, it's in spite of the system, not because of it. It's because the person decides that they're going to do something for himself during that time period. Even the nonsense of maybe losing the university program – the fight and the struggle to keep it – just so that we can educate ourselves. Taxpayers cry because we're getting university education. Some of them claim, well look this prisoner's getting a university education, and I can't afford to send my daughter. Well, let me tell you that it costs … I don't know the exact figures, but something like seven dollars per man, per hour, more to put them in a shop than it does to put them in a classroom. If they think that the prison industry system is there to make money and help them pay for the cost of their incarceration, they're wrong, because prison industries lose money. And, as I say, it costs more for security to keep them locked in their cells than it does to put them in a classroom. You can put twenty or thirty prisoners, students, in a classroom under the supervision of one person. You put them in any other area, and you're dealing with a much lower ratio – you don't have twenty or thirty to one.

I want nothing to do with society at all any more. Once you've been convicted by the courts and turned over to the penitentiary system, you now come under different legislation, as they take away many of the rights that ordinary citizens have, besides the right of freedom, which naturally has to be taken away. I'm not suggesting that I shouldn't be in prison – I killed somebody. Yes, I should be doing time for it.

UPDATE

Al was very involved with inmate politics at William Head, serving on the Inmate Committee. He still believed he would die in prison, felt remorse for his victim's family, but not for the man, who "needed to die." RPC wasn't on his agenda ("they can't force you to go"): he had been "kicked in the nuts" when sentenced and had no intention of pursuing the fifteen-year judicial review ("can you please do it again?", is how he mockingly termed the whole process). He had seen one of his sons for the first time a year ago and had found it very traumatic (it "tears at me"), though he now sees him on a regular basis. He lamented the cancellation of the SFU Prison Education Program in 1992 and the loss of its forty job placements, "There's nothing to do in this jail." The GP and PC populations were not integrated at William Head, and the fact that the former was getting smaller had only served to exacerbate matters. He had managed to reach "Club Fed", but it was still the "end of the line": there was a graveyard out back so they wouldn't need to contact his family. When asked about his plans, he replied, "Do a whole lot of time and then die. Why would I want parole? Freedom doesn't exist for a parolee." He had met a "young lady" before he had left Kent and "got burnt bad" and vowed "never to be vulnerable again." His philosophy was "to get up and see what the day will bring." He joked that in the end the prison might have to throw him out and he'd win by default.

BRUCE

'That's what I'd like to see – a vacation.'

Bruce was twenty-five when sentenced to life-25. He had served six years at the time of this interview.

It's more civilized here [Matsqui]. There seems to be a lot more going on, more activities. Livelier atmosphere than the other ones – Dorchester and Atlantic Institution. Yeah, really tight there. It was tense, very tense all the time. It was like something going to break loose, or people freak out. It was a rough atmosphere to live in.

It was kind of a shock, coming here. I was thinking about going to Kent … max, eh. I was thinking about that for a week or two after coming here, and then I said, oh, it ain't too bad. It's just a lot livelier than the other place was. Seem to be a lot more going on. Seem more civilized.

I kept to myself quite a bit, the first year here, and sort of felt things out and I really chose my friends. Was pretty lucky, I think. People that belong to the chapel, we got to be pretty good friends. Guys been doing the same sentence I'm doing, and it helped me out quite a bit.

Short-termers? Well, they talk a lot, a lot about, oh, getting out and what they're going to be doing. Like, I'm happy for them that they'll be getting out, eh, but they rattle on about it too much and then it's … then you see them coming back. Now, that's really hard. I'll just say – See ya. Not goodbye. Just say see ya.

If I was, you know, if I was in their shoes, just complaining all the time, you know, those short guys, just complaining about the food, and the way things are, and just going on and on about it – and, they get out, and a little while later, they're back. And, see, if I was them, you know, complaining so much, I'd stay out. Wish I had the chance. I know I could, you know, do it. I've got a good taste of what it's like in here … just about six years in. Since I was twenty-five, I guess.

You know, I had a chance to … this is I think where I started to … what led up to my crime. I was working at a place where they make custom furnishings. I worked there quite a while, but I was commuting about sixty miles one way. I was commuting from the valley, and like I had a chance to get a place to live down there, near the cabinet shop at a boarding house, but found out that I had to stay in a room with another person, eh. I wanted to have a room to myself, so I said, oh, forget this. I'll just travel back and forth. And then it got to be too much. I said, there must be work in the valley, you know? And I knew damn well there wasn't any – not till the harvesting. It's kind of a weird thing, because I was good at what I did and they wanted me to work there. I just felt that it was too much. The commuting.

So, I quit my job at the cabinet place and looked for work in the valley. Couldn't find anything. There was nothing to be had there. So, I went out to my grandfather's cottage. I didn't even ask him if I could stay there because, you know, it was like … just went over and worked. He needed a lot of work done around there. And I think that's when it started. I started to really withdraw into myself. Shutting out the outside world.

Like, I started going to town once in a while to look for work. Not really looking, but glancing over the boards at Manpower, but I couldn't find anything that was really good.

Well, I had a little bit of money. Wasn't much but … like, I was looking after my grandfather's car at the time. He was sick, in the hospital, and I was putting all the money I did get into the car, upkeep of the car, gas, and that. Not looking after myself very good.

Well, my uncle and my aunt came down to the cottage and told me to, you know, look for work, and like, they were kicking me off the property. They thought, which it was, they thought it was a good idea to get me out of there, and they said, we're taking the car because your grandfather might need it when he gets well. Like it was a shock because I thought I was looking after that car really good and I was looking after the cottage really good, eh. Put in a lot of work over there and it came to me as a shock. But I understood what they were doing. So, the next day I left there. It was really hard.

They said that I could live with my other uncle in the valley and look for work there, but only for three days, and then I had to find my own place and not live off my uncle. So I did find work, oh, about seven days later I guess it was. I found work – two jobs, pruning apple trees and unloading, loading trucks.

So, I lived there, eh. I lived at his place. They didn't mind, like I was paying them board and everything and helping out around the house. They liked my company so I stayed there. It must have been a couple of weeks or something. And I was bicycling to work, pruning trees and that. Then, I had some kind of problem there. One hot, sunny day I was kind of daydreaming, thinking there's got to be something better. I could pack up and, you know, go west or something. Then, like, the guy who owned the land came along and told me I wasn't doing a very good job. He went and talked to the foreman there. And I said, well, I'm going to quit if I'm not doing a good job.

Having a hard time putting it all together . …

So, I sold my guitar and went. Started hitchhiking out west. I went to Prince Edward Island for a few days, blew just about all my money. And said, I can't go west, I haven't got any money. So I decided to go back to the valley and earn some money. I started hitchhiking back. Time I got back to my grandfather's cottage it was about three o'clock in the morning. So I just stayed over there. Nobody knew I was there because I told everybody I's going out west.

I ran out of food, ran out of money. I broke into the neighbour's cottage, found some food. I did that for a couple of days, eating their food. I noticed there was a box of shotgun shells up on the cupboard there. I said, oh, they keep a shotgun around. Found the shotgun and took that and took a little bit more food and went back to the cottage. I's thinking, this could be a way of getting out of here and getting some money and some food.

The owners of the cottage came over one night and said, we're missing a shotgun and some food. You haven't seen any strange people around? I said no, and they left.

I kept taking their food. Well they locked their door up, but, I knew they probably had the key under their ledge. I found the key and stole some more food. Then they took the key, so I kicked the door down and took the rest of the food.

Now about this time, like, I started thinking that the first person who came down I'd kill and take their car and money and … they [the neighbours] would come down every now and then. I was thinking of killing them and taking their money and car, but every time they did come down I couldn't bring myself to do it. Each time I failed that, I was getting more mad at myself, right?

So I decided it would be a good idea if I took a tent and camped in the woods, because I felt it was getting a little bit hot around there. I think they were getting the idea that I was the one who was breaking in. Well, I put my tent in the woods there, and stayed overnight there. I had a hiding place where I was going to stop the first person who came down, and take their car, and that. But there was, uh . .... I sort of skipped a spot.

There was a time there that I ... that everything just sort of cleared up and I stopped myself and said, what am I doing? I had a sawed-off shotgun in my hand; I had planned to kill ... I don't think I had thought about killing someone then. I had thought of just robbing them. And then, I guess, I broke in their cottage and said, this is really bad. I should stop, but I felt it was too late to stop. Should just get out of there. So I said, I might as well go all the way.

So I was in the woods there and I said, this is it. Tomorrow I'm doing to do it. Whoever comes down, no matter who it is. It ended up, like, I went up to my hiding place there and I saw a fellow walking down, coming towards me, walking by. It was my uncle. He was whistling a tune, and walked by and went down to the cottage. He was calling out for me. And I was thinking, Should I or shouldn't I kill him? I knew he had a car further up the road there. And I was still going back and forth like that. Even when I heard him coming back up.

Hurried around and looked for sort of another hiding place. Chose my old one again. And, uh, as soon as he got up beside me, I jumped out, and held him at gunpoint. He asked me what I was doing. And I said, I don't know why I said this, but I said, I just want to get myself put away for a long time. He said, you're surely going to do that. We talked for, oh, about a half-hour, and then I felt he was just stalling for time or something. He went down on his knees, and I, you know, shot him in the chest. He rolled over and I got him in the upper back. Dragged him into the woods. Probably wasn't dead. Shot him in the back of the head. Took the car and headed out west. Out to northern BC.

Like, my mother, at that time, she was living about sixty miles outside of Fort St. John. They say I was going up to see her, but I went up there because there was a forest fire in the area and I tried to get on that. But by the time I got up there it was out. They had it under control, so there was no work there. I was just about ready to take off again early in the morning and they got me.

But like, when he passed down the sentence there, it was, it was a heavy-duty shock. I was in shock. I was just quiet. I couldn't really, you know, visualize it.

Like, I knew what I did. Like, the crime that I was charged with was premeditated murder, and that's what it was. I knew it was. It was a little bit of premeditation. He judged correctly, for sure.

Yeah. Like I was all set to do that all in Dorchester. I was all psyched up and ready to roll, do the whole thing. I set my mind on, like, I'm just going to live one day at a time and treat this as a good chance to learn stuff, get a trade there, schooling, and stuff.

Oh, I had no idea what it was like in Canadian prisons, eh. Like, I seen Dorchester when we went by going back to Ottawa at Christmas time by train. My father said, that's Dorchester Penitentiary. Gruesome-looking place! And I saw a lot of prison shows, movies, on American TV and that, and said, yow! Thought it was like that.

There's people who did time in jails here and told me all what it was like, eh. But they were wrong. They hadn't been back there for a few years or so.

I didn't really know what to think. Like, when I first walked up the steps, you know, I was thinking I was not going to see the outside again, so I looked around and looked at the valley there, and turned around and walked upstairs and got processed. And when I got to the step where it opens up to the population there, wow! Chicken cages piled on top of each other. Well, here goes! I was really nervous for a while, there.

Well, you hear a lot about, you know, young guys becoming kids for older cons. And a lot of killings going on, and rapes – a lot of gruesome stuff.

So I was, like, making sure I saw nothing – blind eye. Like, I knew you keep to yourself. When you see, you know, you see something going down, turn a blind eye. Say nothing. Hear nothing.

I seen these guys doing big time, you know. I worried about those guys. You just watch what you say. Talk about the weather, fishing, or something. You don't talk to the guards.

Yeah. Like guys have left me alone, I guess because the time I's doing. There's this thing going around the prison. Like, he's doing life, you know, so he doesn't care what happens. He'll take you out at the blink of an eye. I probably survived pretty good on that.

The institution sees me? Real quiet I guess and, like, I guess they're waiting for me to break. I don't, you know, cause them any trouble. Keep to myself. They're wondering, When's he going to blow up?

The family's been really supportive … like, that's what got me through. One sister, she's two years younger, she's up in northern BC. I've only been here for a year and my sister has been down a couple of times already. There was always, seemed to me, a letter, or a card or something, would come, just at the right time.

And well, there's a little bit of the chapel program and a hobby shop. I do woodworking, portraits the odd time, and cards, and calligraphy. I got my Grade 12.

Yeah. I'm working at vocational carpentry here. A really good course. Then, after that, well during that I guess, I'm going to get into drafting – go as far as I can with that. I'm planning on getting the most educated I can get. Get some trades under my belt, so that I can get a good job when I get out.

Yeah. I've got a lot of hope in that fifteen-year thing there.

And I want to just be working at a job that I'm good at – drafting, or woodworking. Cabinetmaking or something. Like, I could be a skilled labourer but I'd like to learn how to be a cabinetmaker.

Well, now I finish things I start. That's a change. Like, before, something goes wrong, I used to drop it and get another job. But I've, like, I've set myself a goal of finishing something I start. And I did pretty good.

I guess the biggest thing would be having my own time to myself, quiet time, playing the guitar, and … something I really miss is privacy. I really miss that.

I try to teach guys manners. Like, friends of mine, eh. I say, well, knock before you come in the door. Like, I've always said, thank you, please, and excuse me, and that. Privacy is one of the biggest things I miss.

Really hard to find. Like, it all bogs down sometimes. Some days it gets really hard and you want to just get away, so you go to your cell and lay down and listen to music. There's this guy I've been listening to since I first started my bit, *Disc Drive*, Jürgen Gothe. I listen to it all, all along, eh. I put that on at four o'clock there or three-thirty and just shut out everything. That's my private moments.

Go to the chapel. Play the guitar once in a while. Sing, talk, and usually one of the guys volunteers something to share out of the Bible. It's great down there.

I have a fellow who comes in every other Monday – eight or nine months, I think – and I'm getting to know him pretty good.

Oh, well first of all, well, how was your week? You know, any trouble, and that? We share. I ask him about his weekend, Anything exciting happen? He asks me, I say, oh, same old thing.

Change anything? A vacation. It'd be like, going out somewhere. Not really going out, just time off. Like, you can do it now, for a day or two, but that's not like an earned vacation. You work for a whole year straight, a week off, and work two years at some job or something, couple of weeks off.

The way they run day-to-day life in here really gets to a person. Routine. Like, if they gave you the option, if you wanted to, you could go over to one of the private family houses, stay there a few days because that really helps a lot. Quiet time. You need a break in the routine. Gets really monotonous sometimes and just gets heavy.

That's what I'd like to see … a vacation.

UPDATE

When contacted five years later about a follow-up interview, Bruce simply replied, "I don't have anything more to say about that, I've said all I have to say."

PHIL

'I'm able to accept that I've done it now – it's out in the open.'

*Phil was twenty when sentenced to life-
25. He had served six years at the time of
his interview.*

I was in Oakalla for thirty-three months before I came to Kent, and
it's kind of weird how you actually get used to it. Oakalla was a real
shit-hole. The staff there were sadistic. Generally speaking it was a
pretty strange transition. You're sitting over remand-side and
you've got people telling you: oh wait till you get to Kent – it's this
way, it's that way. You get all these distorted versions of what it's
like. I always assumed it would be more serious – that the staff
would be worse. I had this idea the staff would be worse in a federal
penitentiary than they were at Oakalla. Because if they could get
away with it in downtown Burnaby, what were they going to do out
in the toolies in some little town like Agassiz. I thought it would be
worse than it was. Looking back now I'd have to say I was paranoid.
I came here and they put me in J-Block and everything was different. You know, after thirty-three months of living a certain way, you

know they put you in this place and everything's electric. And you've got this guy coming round and he opens your door slot and asks you if you want some toast. And you don't know if this guy's population or you know, you're totally disoriented. You don't know east from west, north from … you know. Just totally disoriented. They take you at night – I got here at night.

J-Block is the hole. It was really weird – it took a while to get used to, you know. This cleaner, he came one day and my slot was open, and he said to me, you know, he says to me, if you want a TV, you put in a request for one. And I thought, you know, he was putting me on. I thought he was setting me up for some kind of a joke, so I don't want to look stupid, right. But he seemed sincere and he kept pushing it, so I filled one out and a little while later my door opened up and there was a TV sitting on the floor in the hallway, and I thought for sure it must have been a setup. The staff at Oakalla, they would set you up. You know, they'd come on the range, they'd be walking down the tier, and they would go in your cell for what they call a cell check. At random – they'd just walk in your cell. I was cleaning one day, and I had this staff member … well, I had a problem with this particular staff member because I was instrumental in getting him a twenty-two-day suspension without pay because he assaulted a prisoner, and I called the ombudsman's office. Anyways, the police were in, the guy got a transfer and everything. Yeah, he went in my cell, and he left. I went out for a little bit of exercise in this gymnasium area upstairs – Southwing Obs [Southwing Observation, where dangerous offenders were under 24-hour surveillance] – and then they called me in the office and asked me if this little bag was mine. I had this canvas bag – book bag – and I said, yeah, and there was one of the top guys there, I guess he's called an SCO, a senior corrections officer. And I said, yeah. And he said: what's in the bag, and I said, books. And he said, well, what else? And I said, nothing. And he said, what about this – and he pulled out a shank! Yeah, I couldn't believe it. I looked over his shoulder at the staff member that was in my cell prior to that, and he's got a smirk on his face. The other guy, the SCO, he can't see that – he's doing his paperwork and here's this guy smirking. Anyways, I couldn't believe that place.

I was originally charged with first-degree murder and I was arrested in July of '84. I went for a thirty-day psychiatric remand at the Forensic Psychiatric Institute at Coquitlam, and then in August '84 I went to Oakalla, and I was there until April of '87. I was convicted – of first-degree. They kept me in the maximum-security wing at Oakalla in Southwing Obs. And all I had to do was to have my lawyer go to court and ask to have my provincial remand changed to a federal remand, and I'd be sent here, because I was doing a life sentence. But I had a hard time letting go of the people, and I was so close to town – I had friends and people coming in, and relatives coming visiting me. I had really good phone access and I did find out one piece of information that was true – that the phone access at Kent is a lot less than it is at Oakalla. I could talk for two hours if I wanted to. Here it's a lot harder for people to visit you and you get one phone call a week if you're lucky, ten minutes. I found that I wrote more for a while than I normally did. And then you find that because there's more programs here you get so absorbed in that that you can eventually … you actually become antisocial.

For the most part the programs you're involved in are just with other prisoners. And you have the odd outside visitor and stuff, but they're not people that are dealing with you on a personal level, as much as they are providing a service. It's hard to get close to them on a personal level. And so, you're isolated from the people that you're close to, you're isolated from people who know who you are from being out there. You're close to people who come to know you in here. I'm at the point now when I don't miss visits. I don't miss phone calls, I don't look forward – actually I find visits kind of uncomfortable, to tell you the truth. Especially the socials when the people come to the institution. I never thought it would get like that.

I'm involved in Native Brotherhood activities. I was voted in as president of the Native Brotherhood. My brothers were having a hard time getting their spirituality recognized, and getting a sweat lodge, which is the equivalent of a church. We've got that now – a couple of years of writing letters and getting MPs and people on their case, they finally came through with it.

I was adopted into a Caucasian family and lived in a mostly Caucasian community, and I went to this elementary school, and for the most part I got along, but the odd kid would make fun of me. You know, kids will be kids – and kids can be cruel sometimes – and the odd kid would make a remark or something. I got involved in drugs in about Grade 9. I started using drugs. I had poor family relationships and the whole family structure was messed up – it was falling apart. My adopted mother was a manic-depressive and my father was an alcoholic, and there were some serious problems there, and I developed my own problems as a result of that situation. I have an uncle – well he's not really my uncle, but my adoptive father's younger brother – saw the situation and asked if I wanted to live with him and his wife up in northern BC. So, I went up there and lived there and completed Grade 11. But then the drugs and things – I still had those problems. Yeah, I had a hard time getting close to people, for the most part. I had friends, what I would call friends, but I had a hard time really trusting people and my relationships with women were basically superficial for the most part. There was one relationship I had with an older woman, she was ten years my senior and she became overly serious, and I was only sixteen and I just couldn't deal with it. I completed Grade 11, and because of this problem that developed I had to get away from where I was. I was doing firefighting and I was doing some different jobs there. I moved into town with this guy was a janitor at the school. I found out he was a homosexual and at that time in my life I couldn't deal with that. I had an extreme prejudice. I had to move away. So, I moved back down to Surrey. The same thing happened again – I figured, you know, a year and a half away from the situation, I was going to mature and I was going to become a different person. You know, in a month or two, it was the same scenario, it was the same bullshit … the fighting, the violence.

A funny thing happened the other day. I received a birthday card from, of all people, my adoptive mother and it infuriated me so. I couldn't believe the anger that I felt. I expressed my desire not to have any contact with these people. I don't want anything to do with them. I have bitter memories of my childhood and I'm not able to forgive yet … not just able to … maybe some day I will, but right now, you know, I've got to get my act together before I can do it. I couldn't believe the anger that … that came out of me. There was no return address so I didn't know who it was from. I opened it up and saw this birthday card: Happy Birthday, Son! And I took a pen and I was jamming it in the paper and I was scribbling the words out … all the sweet-sounding words, sugar-coated words, and I took whiteout and dumped it on there and smeared it around. I took … I took pens, inks, colours … I completely destroyed this card. I scrubbed off the Carleton Cards off the back and I wrote Eat Shit Cards, and I crumpled it up, folded it up, typed out a letter. I didn't personalize it by putting any of my handwriting on it; I just typed my initials and I wrote: Dear Mom – or I didn't write "dear", I just said, please do not send any more mail this way, you have no relatives here. Thank you for fucking off. And I sent it. And I thought about it after. I thought, why did I do that? Where's this anger coming from? And, I couldn't believe, I couldn't believe this anger that I had. It was infuriating.

I've realized now, you know, after six years, that I've still got a hell of a lot of anger inside of me. And, I'm not sure where it all stems from, how it could all be there after all this time. But I know that, know that it's that kind of anger that allowed me to do what I did. Well … you know, I've been told different things. The police tell me I'm a psychopath, my psychologist tells me I've got episodic dyscontrol syndrome. I don't really ... I don't really know. You know, I can say that I never thought I was capable of doing what I did. I can say that, up to the point where this crime happened. I had never before conceived that I would be capable of doing that. I mean, I've been angry, I've gone to the bar, and I've drunk and I've got in fights. I've actually gone to the bars and looked for fights. I've gone out of my way to create fights.

I picked her up hitchhiking. It was kind of ironic – I always pick up hitchhikers. Especially female hitchhikers for various reasons. If I was single at the time, it was a good way to meet women. Two – the main reason – you know you read in the papers all these things that happen and you think, well, if I don't pick this lady up, some creep might pick her up, you know, some dangerous person might pick her up. And it was raining and I was supposed to be returning home from a nightclub and she was hitchhiking in the rain, so I picked her up. She expressed a desire not to go home; she wanted to go park. I took it as a come-on. I parked. I had some beer, we drank a few beers. I had done some cocaine that evening and I was pretty high, but I was feeling good, I didn't feel ... didn't feel angry inside. I made a sexual advance towards her and she rejected it – and I exploded. I ... this anger came out of me like ... I saw pictures of it after. I had pieces of recollection of it, but I don't remember anything that happened. Her neck was broken in several places. It was horrible. I never thought I was capable of doing that. You know, you always have these situations – you go out, you get drunk, the next morning you wake up and you have this guilty feeling that you did something, and it's done. And you start thinking what was it ... and you think, oh no, and you check your wallet – did I spend a whole paycheque? You check your wallet – okay, that's fine. Oh no, how did I get home? You check your car for dents. Did I smash my car up, did I scrape my paint? I woke up the next morning – I had this horrible, horrible ... I can't even begin to describe it. And I had a vague recollection of what took place. I hoped to hell it was a dream. I went to my car, and saw her purse in my car. From that point on I was not the same person. From that point on, I didn't know who I was. I went into the car. This can't be happening, I kept telling myself this can't be happening. I opened the purse, and there's ID – I can see a picture – I remembered the face – there's a pair of shoes in my car … you know … there's just a … I couldn't believe it. My girlfriend's in the house. I'm a murderer. I committed murder – I couldn't believe it. I can't explain it – you know, your head just reels – your head, your head just reels. It was like I could never conceive of this happening, but it happened. And now I was the one … I was the one. All those things I had read in the paper before – of all the people who had done those crimes – now I was one of them. And I didn't know how to categorize myself, I didn't know how to identify with myself. What does it mean to be caught? Okay, well every person in your life is going to know. Every person that knows you is going to know that you did this. Every person is going to read about it in the paper. Every person is going to hate you. They're all going to hate you … and I was always the one, you know, because of the sensitivity of my childhood, the situation at home. I was always put down and stuff, I was always worried about what people thought. I always had to work for people's favour. And now, and now, I was going to destroy everything, every bond I had ever made with people. You know, there's nothing you can do, there's absolutely nothing. I hadn't heard anything in the papers, I hadn't read anything. I hadn't seen anything, I hadn't received any other sources of information about what took place. I tried to keep it all together while I thought what to do. I thought about turning myself in, but I didn't have what it took to turn myself in. I don't know what it takes to turn yourself in, but you're going to go to the police and you're going to say, look, I've committed a murder. I just wasn't able to do it. There was just too much happening in my head. I can't describe it, I can't describe it. I was afraid to turn myself in. I had … I had false ideas of prison. I had false ideas of what was going to take place from there on – I had false ideas about the law. I had no idea what was going to happen from then on. I had no tangible way to grab a hold of it. You see this is the part that really, that really fucks my head. I told myself over the next couple of days, there's no way I can turn myself in. I didn't have what it took to commit suicide. I thought about that, I had a rifle, I fondled it, I put it to my head – I fondled it, I didn't load it, but I just wanted to see – I got as close as I was able to without letting myself commit suicide – and I thought about it. I played with the trigger, and I wanted to see what it would feel like, and I imagined loading it, and I imagined doing it – and that's the first step, you know. You know you have to think about it first, and I wasn't able to do it. I thought that, I thought that somehow what had taken place was a result of the cocaine. It's not me, because I could never think of this kind of thing.

I did my best to keep it together, and I managed to get my life relatively back on track. I continued working, but people were commenting about my attitude at work. People were finding me standing in a corner staring off out the window, blind-faced. They'd wave their hand in front of my face and I snapped to it, and they'd ask me what was wrong and I'd lie to them, and say I was just thinking about something. I'd be doing dishes and my girlfriend would come in, and then she'd leave and she'd come back a minute later and I'd be bawling my eyes out and she'd ask me what was wrong – and I'd say I was thinking about the way I treated my mother as a child, or something. And I lied to everybody. And I tried everything I could to keep it under. I know this is ironic – this is really ironic – I went for a drive one night. I hopped in my car, and I just went for a long drive. I don't know what, why, where I was going – whatever – but I drove from Langley. I drove up through Abbotsford and through Mission, past Hemlock Valley. I found myself on the road to Harrison Hot Springs, and I drove down the hill from the old way – not the highway but from Mission – I was coming down the hill, and I saw all these yellow lights in this government complex thing, and I remember distinctly thinking to myself: What is that, what is that, and I thought it must be some kind of a powerplant or some kind of a government place, and it was Kent Max, of course. But I drove by, I went to Harrison Hot Springs, and I was having all kinds of really schizophrenic delusions – I had this idea that, that I was going to go to Harrison Hot Springs, and that when I was walking around on the beach I had this idea that, you know, that this hand of a dead person was going to come out of the sand and start dragging me down.

I'm able to accept that I've done it now – it's out in the open now. There's nothing to hide now. In the sense that whatever it is I have to talk about, I can talk about. Before I didn't know who to tell and what I would say if I told them. But now, people come to me and if I want I can have a psychologist talk to me and explain things. I have no use for the institutional psychologist. Anyways, I do have some faith in psychology – I have nowhere else to go for answers anyway, other than spirituality and really that doesn't give you answers.

Coming to prison has probably been the best thing that ever happened to me. I don't know what else to say. Coming to prison, I've discovered my culture, I've discovered my heritage. The way of Native people, and I didn't have that. And now I feel closer to home. I feel I have more of an identity restored. A different identity than I had before. I mean, I can't even relate to the person that I was before. I didn't have any confidence in my ability at all – I had no use for education. I'm actually enjoying my education now; I'm enjoying learning now.

I can't grasp the sentence. You're speaking of life-25 – this is kind of coincidental that this interview is taking place now – a short time ago my life-25 was quashed – I won my appeal. I was convicted of the first-degree, and then I had the sentence thrown out. Because of some problems, some things the police did, the way trial proceeded – the judge made some errors. I'm not a lawyer. I've got a new trial on the first-degree. What we were trying to prove at the first trial was whether or not I fully appreciated the nature and quality of the actions at the time of the offence. Now, I was doing cocaine and I'm on alcohol, and I've got some obvious psychological problems that the doctors are still trying to pinpoint. Life-25 really means that you are eligible for parole in twenty-five years, it doesn't mean they're going to give it to you. So, I could be doing anywhere from life in prison, to the end of my new trial. I mean, I could win my new trial. My new trial will probably take place in a year and a half, two years, and a win could be anything from getting a second-degree to manslaughter.

What were my reactions when I received the life-25 sentence? That's a tough one. I prepared myself. I was sitting in there, I knew the judge was out, I knew the jury was out deliberating. I knew that sooner or later they were going to come in and they were going to say … one of many things. They were going to say: guilty of first-degree; guilty of second-degree; guilty of manslaughter; guilty of, what-do-you-call-it, guilty of involuntary manslaughter; or voluntary manslaughter; or possibly a not guilty due to insanity; a not guilty due to drunkenness; not guilty due to various other reasons. I thought, what would I feel? And of course I could never know what I would feel until it happened – so, I just sort of waited till it happened. And I sat in there and, of course, I was convicted of first-degree, and they said life-25, and I waited for the jury to say guilty of first-degree. I knew there was only one sentence that the judge could pass and that was life-25, the maximum. But of course he has to say it, so I sat there and I thought I would feel what I was supposed to feel when the jury said it, but I didn't, didn't really feel anything. It was almost as if I knew that that was what I was going to be convicted of. And it wasn't a surprise and I sat there, and I waited for the judge to say the sentence and when he said the sentence, I expected the feeling to hit me then, and when he said it, for a brief second, it was like I was the only one in the room and then it seemed like I was the only one not in the room. It was nothing. It was totally beyond my control. I was just sitting there hearing it, and I could have been watching a movie. I can't really explain what I felt. I don't think I felt anything. It was just beyond me because I couldn't comprehend it.

I am coming closer to comprehending it. I've done six now, and so I can figure, well, twelve … and then six months … three times what I've just done … more to go. And in that sense I can sort of see it numerically, but in seeing how much I've changed in the six years that I've been in here I can't comprehend. How I would be in another six times three. I can't imagine, I can't imagine that. But that's only the twenty-five, that's not to say that I'm going to get out in twenty-five. If you did win that option to apply for the judicial review, if you did win and you had eligibility reduced, they can still deny it for the rest of your life. So, a life-7, life-10, life-15, life-25 … really, it all boils down to how you're perceived by them. I've had other prisoners tell me they can't understand how a person like me ended up in prison. You know, how a person like me did what I did, and I tell them I don't know how I did it either. Then there's other people who think they know why I did what I did.

In this situation there is no definition of who's going to associate with whom. In PC, people just disregard what somebody's done. For the most part they disregard what somebody's done, and they just deal with them as a person. Because everybody's in PC for one reason or another. There has been the odd person who's been sent in from general population situations for a gambling debt, or something – and these are the loud-mouths that yell out of the windows: Ah, you PC scumbags, whatever, you know. The next thing you know they're in, they're in PC and they're looking at you face to face, and they don't say a word. They don't say a word, it's always the loud ones too, you know – always the real loud ones – and then they're in PC and then they're real quiet because, they know, they see it that some of the guys in PC could do damage if they wanted to. You have to establish your own sort of status, or space to live in. It is a lot different than I thought it would be. I had no idea what it would be like. No one who has never been in prison can say they know what it's like to be in prison.

I hate to say it but the truth of the matter is, that the one thing that works best in prison is violence. If you want people to respect your space then they have to fear you to some extent or other. And that's a sick reality of prison. I hate to say it, but I think that a person could become far more dangerous living in a place like this for a prolonged period of time, than he would if they were dealt with in some other fashion. What I'm saying here is if I had stayed out there, and if I had eluded the police and managed to escape, whatever, I was so messed up from what I was doing and knowing who I was and everything that I cannot say that I wouldn't have done it again, and I suspect I probably would have. I know that if I was given the chance I wouldn't use drugs or alcohol again. In prison, despite the drugs and alcohol, I avoid any kinds of mind-altering substances that would render you incapable of controlling yourself. I know I've got anger inside of me and I know I have to deal with it and, if I use drugs like that, it's going to come out.

If you want prison to be a place where you're going to put people and keep them there so they don't cause any harm to society, then you put them there and you just don't let them out. I think, to an extent, prison is good for just about anybody, to an extent, because it gives a person a chance to step out of the situation he was in and get an objective perspective of the way things were, his life, society, from a sort of objective perspective. They get a chance to work on themselves; they got a lot of solitude, a lot of time to think. And I think a couple of years, three, four years tops, you're getting into a grey area. After that I think what happens is a decline from there on. I think the negative attributes of prison then overcome anything that you can do positive with yourself.

I think the main thing is with your crime, I think that you have to understand it. Okay, first of all, you have to understand the crime, why you did what you did. Second of all, you have to have some self-respect. Now, if you don't have any self-respect, it doesn't matter what you know because, if you don't respect yourself, you're not going to respect anybody else. And if society rejects you, puts you in a situation like this, where you're away from them and you're not wanted, that's the ultimate rejection. And maybe in that respect, maybe I did that to myself on purpose. Maybe I wanted this to happen. I don't know, I'm not a psychologist. After a point you just collect dust, and it's all negative.

Violence in prison is used as a tool to protect yourself, but I think there comes a point where that's all you are: you're somebody that's feared in prison, or somebody that is respected. You're not really respected, but in a sense you are, you're respected because of how much fear you instill in others. People tend to gravitate towards those that are the most dangerous because they'd rather be close to you than on the other side of you, so you have a psychological advantage, and you can do easier time. But, that's the wrong kind of socialization, you don't want to take that to the street. If I was going to make changes with prison, I would change the whole system. If I had, all of a sudden, boom, the power to change everything, it would be as much like society as possible with just stricter control. Maybe it's totally contradictory, maybe it could never happen or maybe I'm talking Big Brother here, I don't know, but we've got a lot of technology, we've electronic wristbands, legbands, whatever, you've medication you can take so that if you take drugs or alcohol it would make you sick. There are ways of doing this, you could probably put more responsibility on your family and friends, people who do care about you, people who do come in and visit you. But if prison's going to be a warehouse, then it should be a warehouse, but you can't have a warehouse of reform, because the two terms are mutually exclusive. You have to decide who has to be warehoused, and who has to be given another chance.

What would I want to do when I get out of the prison? That's a very tough question. I'd like to pursue a career in Native politics. I don't know anything about my biological parents, but I know about the Native people, and I know how the Europeans came over here, and sort of basically took over the place, and how society is polluting our planet, and how the fish are dying, and how the trees are being cut down and how everything is being polluted, and I don't know how people can expect it to go on like this. It can't go on like this. I'm trying to find my biological parents, so I have to send away for my birth certificate to get certain information, and they send me a birth certificate with my adoptive parents' names on it as my parents! Coming here, and learning about it, learning about my culture, learning about what happened, learning about why there are so many Natives in prison. A lot of these guys, most of the Natives in here that I know, we have this Native drug and alcohol awareness program – just about 99 percent of the Natives that are in prison are in as a result of alcohol and/or drugs. It was involved in the crime to one extent or another, and to see them and to meet them and to talk to them, they don't seem like the kind of people that would do the things that they've done. I've gained a lot of pride, I've gained a lot pride in the culture. I've gained a new sense of identity, and now I've got something to sort of fight for, because I can see how my people have been hurt in a lot of ways, and are still being hurt.

I'm not going to give up hope at this point. I'm going to just keep trying to do whatever it is I'm doing, just wait for the new trial, and wait for things to happen, and at that point, I'll have to sort of get a grip on things. Whatever happens, happens. I think if I stayed in prison for even twenty years I would be far more dangerous than I was when I was arrested. I see that definitely happening. Becoming more dangerous, because I never thought that I'd get to the point where I wouldn't miss visits, and now I'm at the point where I don't even like visits. I'm not saying I don't need people. I think everybody needs people, everybody needs to feel loved, but you get to a point in prison where you become sort of callous, you become sort of desensitized to that sort of thing, and I think after a certain point you can never reawaken that.

UPDATE

When Phil was interviewed again in the summer of 1995 at RPC (Matsqui), he was only a few weeks away from finishing his program there. He sang the praises of the personality disorder program – "it really works" – particularly the empathy and role-play module, which had enabled him to see the situation from his victim's perspective. He was worried about having to return to his "parent institution" (Kent); he didn't want to go back there because it was "so negative, you'd unlearn positive things learned here." He stated that he "feels good now, the pressure is off."

Phil said that a lot had happened since his first interview: shortly afterwards, his first-degree murder conviction had been quashed and a new trial was originally scheduled for 1991. The trial, however, did not take place: "The 'deal' was that I plead guilty to second-degree murder and accept a life sentence with a fifteen-year minimum before parole eligibility. The Crown Prosecutor made it clear that if I refused the deal, went to trial and successfully proved manslaughter, he would work to have me declared a dangerous offender. A DO hearing is not like a trial; the Crown does not need evidence to prove what he is purporting. The bottom line was, I would have been accused of things I could not disprove, and my lawyers felt that, given the amount of time I have already served [eleven years as of this update], I am better off with a life-15 than I am with a manslaughter conviction and a dangerous offender label."

BURR

'Nobody really knows who I am. Neither do I.'

Burr was thirty years old when sentenced to life-25. He had served six years at the time of this interview.

My last actually completed grade in school was, I believe, the sixth grade. I was born in Winnipeg. We stayed there for a year, and after my dad left we moved to Victoria, my mom and I. Then when I was about ten, my mom and I moved to the States, to California. We were only in California for about a month and then we moved to Washington, DC on the East Coast. We stayed in DC for about four years. And about that time Mom got involved with music (she's a lyricist, eh). She's good with words. So she got involved with that and then she got involved with bookkeeping for a chain of restaurants called Mr. Henry's. I, from about age ten, because Mom was so involved with those things, buggered off to a military school for two years. That's when I realized I didn't want to get involved with the service.

After that, there was really no school, you know. I was really, more or less, kind of the house pet-type trip, eh? You know, like I'd go down to one restaurant and then I'd go over to the other restaurant. The darling of the crowd kind of shit, eh?

Two years later, Mom moved down to California and I was still living in DC with my godfather. Mom was down in California, because they put out a record, eh? And, I don't know, I didn't really like that separation. The only tie with any kind of family that I've had was me and Mom. And when you took that away, I floundered; I … where the hell am I? I became frightened. So, I basically told my godfather, this was at about fourteen, listen, I've got to go. He didn't really like the idea of me just up and leaving, but that's what I did.

Left. Travelled across the country. Hitchhiked. From the letters that had come in to the various people in the restaurants, I had Mom's address. It took me a while but I tracked her down and just one day showed up at the door. It was knock, knock, knock, hi, how are you doing. You know she blew her lights. It was interesting.

After that, there were foster homes and boys homes and group homes that were dispersed. I would go to school, but I was bored with school. I never went to a juvenile hall; never did any time in the county jail, with the exception of just going to be processed in. I got involved in all the B&Es and stolen vehicles and whatnot as a juvenile out of boredom. You know, it was just I didn't have anything to do.

I was actually eighteen my first time in. I've only been out four months in 1978. The majority of my time was done down in the States. They didn't really have a pre-release program down there. They just put me on medication. I recently got back on it because I'm finding myself becoming irritated at really stupid things. Things that, if I allowed to go any further, I'd get in more trouble. I was paroled in June of '84 and I was arrested November of '84 for the current charge – murder.

The problem basically was when you go from 2,000 milligrams a day of Chloropromazine or Thorazine (the basic bug juice, eh) to nothing – no outpatient care, no contact whatsoever in the community. It didn't take but about three weeks for the withdrawals to start. And then any kind of pressure just added to that, it just escalated.

I was basically taken from Vacaville in California by the immigration department, to the airport, put on a plane, dropped off at the Vancouver airport and that was it. The first thing that affected me was the culture shock. I had been taken from behind a thirty-foot wall and dropped off at the Vancouver International Airport. They sent me through customs, checked my deportation package, photographed me and told me to run along. And that was it. That's all there was. The problem was ... out amongst the thousands of people ... I was still in a state of shock. And the trees – I mean to be actually able to touch a tree was a novelty to me.

From there ... my grandfather was the only relative that I had in Canada that felt comfortable enough to open his house to me, because I'm more or less the black sheep of the family. But his mind and his attitudes and values are thirty years, forty years old. The last time I had seen him I was twelve years old. I was twenty-five when I was released, eh, and he was still approaching me as if I were still twelve years old, and I think that is where some of the conflict came at home.

I managed to get a job washing dishes, but when I was down in the United States I was a mortician. I worked in a mortuary embalming bodies. I started out basically as a flower driver, moved up to first calls, going out and picking up the bodies, and gathering information and bringing them back, and from there went into embalming and somebody else would go and pick them up and bring them back. I applied at several funeral homes. I had my references, and they said, okay you're qualified, we'll put you on a list and when something comes up, we'll notify you. But in the meantime, I had to work, so the actual first paying job I got was picking raspberries. It was the only thing I was really qualified to do at the time.

From there I got a job washing dishes, and I decided, because of conflicts at home with my grandfather, I decided to get an apartment. And in the process, through my ex-old lady, I got a vehicle. I worked there for about a month. Then the owner and his wife went to Hawaii for a vacation – and when that happened, individuals in the restaurant wanted to go union. We had a meeting and I thought well, if I can get paid seven or eight dollars for washing dishes rather than three dollars, that would be marvellous. So I paid my two dollars dues. The owner came back rather unexpectedly and because I was the last to be hired, I was the first to be fired. He fired about a third of the staff and the rest went. It's been since closed down, eh.

I got fired, went down to Human Resources, and Human Resources said come to see us on this day and we'll assist you, until you can get back on your feet. Missed the appointment by five minutes, was rescheduled two weeks down the road, which of course blew my apartment. I was no longer able to pay for it so I couldn't stay there. So I was basically relegated to the car. The car payment came due. Even though it was paid for I made a verbal agreement with Irene's mother that as I worked I would make the payments to her.

The job was gone, the living space was gone, there was nobody left to talk to, and again the beginning of a psychosis, I guess you could call it, with relation to the lack of medication. Frustration, anger, confusion, culture shock, it all hit at one time. I just didn't know how to deal with it because I had no preparation for it. So I decided I would leave. Again, it was irrational because there was really no thought given to it – it was just flee. That was the basis. Well, when I explained to my ex-old lady that it was time to go, she wanted to go too. So we went. She was seventeen at the time. We ended up up north in the Cariboo area.

The deterioration of mind continued and the stresses of living out in the bush … when I heard my name announced over the radio it threw me off kilter. Irene's mother was looking for us and she'd called the various police agencies and the announcement was basically for us to report to the nearest RCMP detachment – we'd like to talk to you. Well, I had cashed two bogus cheques before we left, to get the car in shape for the trip, and that's what I thought they were referring to. Now because I had just been recently released, I thought, okay, we're pinched because they knew where we were. I decided it was time we go.

During the process of getting out of there, we did a couple of B&Es to gain food, clothing, and as a by-product ran across weapons. During the course of our escape, we ran across Mr. Parks. Mr. Parks, he was a good old gentleman. It's the only way I can explain it. He was no threat. During the course of us relieving him of his vehicle, Irene had laid a weapon down. It was loaded. An argument ensued between Mr. Parks and myself, I don't remember all of it, because at that point I was ... I like to call it tipped ... because I was right to the edge. I wasn't really in contact, just partially. Basically, an argument ensued. He reached for the weapon. I had my weapon, and I can't really explain what went through my mind at that point because there was just mass confusion.

The end result was that the gentleman was on the ground. I had apparently shot him twice. I was numb; there was no emotion. The shock of the whole situation hadn't really hit me at that point. It began to hit me in stages, and as it hit me it was like a sledge hammer knocking me down, eh, because I began to realize just what I had done.

Took his vehicle; escaped Canada; headed down toward California, to Vacaville.

Yeah, I was trying to think why I went there. My mind was in such a confused state that I was trying to get me somewhere I had been before; some place familiar so that I could get this all back into perspective. It was just a panic flee. There was no thought involved. I made many, many mistakes. The SWAT team almost got us a couple of times. It was just a mad, irrational run.

Got down to Oregon. The vehicle was running poorly. We had twenty dollars basically to our name. Got a hotel room. The people who were next door to us ... we ended up robbing them at gun point. Nobody was hurt. One of the things that they commented on when they got into the courtroom was that we were basically very polite. We told them exactly what we were doing and there was no problem, because there was no need for any kind of violence at all. Obtained the money, got down to Vacaville, was arrested promptly thereafter. As a result here I sit doing life-25. Irene was convicted of a lesser charge of armed robbery in Oregon and picked up fifteen months and was released shortly thereafter.

No. I expected it. My lawyer was telling me I wouldn't get life-25. I expected it because I couldn't take the stand. There was nothing I could say that wouldn't incriminate Irene and that goes against my principles. There was no way I could defend myself without involving her in the criminal act. My best defence in my own mind, and I still feel this way, was no defence at all. Let her say whatever she needs to, to get herself off, and I'd just remain silent and take whatever comes, because as I've said, I've never denied that I was responsible for taking the man's life, but I think life-15 for second-degree would have been reasonable. I think that for what I've done in the eyes of society, it's reasonable. In my own mind I'm never going to be able to forgive myself for what I have done, but to say that it was premeditated murder and that it was cold-blooded and that I just did it because I enjoyed it, is just bullshit.

Yeah. I did a year and a half down there in Oregon State Penitentiary for the robberies, before I was able to come back to Canada. It was about three and a half years after I was arrested that I finally went to trial for the murder charge, and I came directly from Oregon State to Kent. I was at Kent for about a year before I went to trial – year and a half. Went. It was two weeks long. I was found guilty of first-degree. The judge excused the jury. My lawyer told the judge that I wanted sentencing now. Life-25. It didn't have a serious impact on me because I had already gone through the emotional turmoil. I knew that life-25 was basically the duration – from now until time ends, right? But I had to accept it in my own mind, or

I wouldn't have been able to deal with it. I had accepted it deep, deep down inside. My main concern was, how am I going to remain myself through that period of time? Am I going to change? And I'm still waiting to see if it's going to be a negative change. I don't think it is.

Yeah. I thought, am I just going to come back and dump somebody because they get in my face? Because now they've taken that restriction away from me. There is no punishment they can give me now that is any worse than the one I have. There's nothing other than myself to stop me from being completely uncivilized. And that pulled me up. That made me stop and think. Because now, why should I get in a fight with somebody? Why not just dump them? I'm being candid with you. Why not just dump them and then I don't have to worry about that any more. What are they going to do? Pick me up, pack my bags and send me to the SHU [Special Handling Unit] for four years? A change of location. I'm still just doing time. But I think about it and I think about how I felt when I finally realized inside what I had done to Mr. Parks. I don't think that feeling would change. I don't think I'd be able to do it again.

No. All my life I've been a pacifist. You know, I don't like violence. I don't like causing people pain or injury. When it happened a portion of me became cold. It was almost as if the whole thing ... I was emotionally detached. I was an observer; I wasn't actually a participant. And when the observer and participant met, that was when I realized up here, and in here, eh, that I'd really done something bad. And there was nothing I could do to change it. The only way that I can deal with this whole situation is to look at it in black and white. I have to deal with reality. If I start to hide, or I start to worry about the things that I can't change, I'll eat myself up. I'll never make it through this.

I made a commitment to myself that I would do the first fifteen years to the best of my ability. I would try to improve my education and gain as many skills as possible; try to get myself into a position where, when I go up to the fifteen-year review, I can say this is what I've done, this is what I've done, and this is what I've done, and not have it be bullshit. I have to prepare. And the only way I can prepare for release or a possible release, fifteen years from now or twenty-five years from now, is to start right now. And I never did that before. Down in the States, I waited until the last year before I really started giving any thought to what I was going to do when I got out, and you can see the result.

You remember when I took the GED program, eh? I didn't need the GED but I wanted to see if all the time that I had done had actually stagnated me that much; if it had pulled me away and isolated me. The simple fact of obtaining the GED allowed me the room to at least think, okay, I can still change, I can still adapt with the times. So because I passed that, I feel confident and it's funny because it's such a simple thing, but I do feel confident that I can make the necessary changes.

Since coming here? There is a change in the sense that in the past I would never think. It would never really occur to me to think about the consequences of what I would do, or plan ahead. Like, to plan ahead for more than six months was a major effort. It was really a major effort. But now I've got the next twenty years planned. In the past I would set goals that were unreasonable, that were unattainable. So I would set myself up for failure. Here, what I've done is I've set up short-term goals and long-term goals, and I've thought about why I want those goals and what they're going to do for me. The end result is that everything that I do, a majority of things that I do, are all geared for when I am separated from the system. Because it's like I have to build a strong foundation now, or I'm not going to be able to build a house on it later on down the road. I never thought like that before.

Now I have the time and so, of course, in order for me to accept this, I have to sit down and … there's really a lot of introspection. I had to sit down and look inside and say, what are you going to do, hang up? Are you going to escape? You know, are you going to lose it and go crazy? What are you going to do? And I had to sit down and think, what is best for me? And that's another thing – I never really put myself first before. It was always, what do you require, what do you require? I'll deal with that and then I'll deal with myself. Now it's, I'll deal with myself and once I've got that taken care of, then I can help you. My priorities have changed just a bit. I've thought more about the future. The future is there. It's uncertain, but it does exist.

One of the things that I found that I've been doing is, I will push 95 percent of what goes on around me away. I won't let it affect me. I don't pay a lot of attention to the things that go on around me. I realize that I'm going to be here. People will go out and either make a good life, or recommit and come back several times before I even become eligible . So I try not to allow anything that happens outside – and I'm talking about on the range, the cell block ... I only know about five or six people on the range that I live on, and I've been living there for a year. The other people, they don't count. They exist, but they have no relevancy.

The majority of the people that I know, that I associate with here, I've known from Kent. And they are people that have basically the same attitude – do your own time. The bottom line is, we don't get involved. I personally try not to get involved in politics, the bullshit, the gangs, the dope – I don't have time for any of that because it's too difficult just to stay sane. Just to be able to get up in the morning and look in the mirror and say, well you've fucked up but, hey, try to do something with it. The other people that I usually associate with, they share the same feelings. It's nice to sit down with just one or two people that you feel comfortable with. When the silences are comfortable, then that's good. It helps.

No. I'll never begrudge an individual the opportunity to get out and go back to society. I feel happy for them. Just because I can't leave doesn't mean that I have to scowl and frown upon everybody else who does get the opportunity. I'm the one that fucked up. I'll feel a sense of loss simply because that was an individual that I could sit down and talk with and be able to relax with. Yeah, it's like adopting a family and losing a member of that family. When it's a friend, I'll feel the loss but I wish him the best and I hope that I never see him again.

Well, I've seen so many of the others come back as repeats, it's difficult for me to visualize. I look at myself – I came back. So I can understand fucking up once, you know there are circumstances that no matter how well you prepare, if those circumstances all hit you at one time, there is nothing you can do. But to go out and come back two months later, stay a month, go out, come back three months later, go out, come back two months later, that's nonsense. I don't want to talk to those people. There's obviously some sort of fault or short-circuiting happening in their head. Maybe they just don't take the situation as seriously as it should be taken.

I've got a slight advantage. My time alone is a buffer zone between me and a lot of the bugs that are running around. When you look at a person who's doing, say ten years, and then you look at a person who's doing life-25 you would prefer, if you're going to fuck with somebody, to fuck with the person who's doing ten years, because they have an out date so subconsciously you think, okay, I might be able to get away with pushing him a little bit farther. But this other guy, he's doing life-25, what's to stop him from killing me? This is the mentality in here. So I think I've got a buffer zone. I can afford to be rude in a polite way. Like, if somebody comes and they're irritating me, I can say, hey listen, don't fuck off mad, just fuck off. I've had a bad day. Get away from me. Usually, if somebody comes to my door, I'm pretty good with the gut feeling. If I talk to somebody for a couple of minutes, I will know whether or not I want to associate with this individual. I don't look at people for what they can do for me, I just look at people who have similar interests, who have similar hurts and are going through similar frustrations.

Well, like I said, I try to keep myself uninvolved with the bullshit, the con artists. I look at it – I've gone through that, I've come to the realization that it's just a useless endeavour; it gets you nowhere. Say I con you today, how is that going to affect me ten years from now? This is something that a person who doesn't have a lot of time … it never occurs to them to think, what are the consequences of what I do today going to be ten years from now? How is it going to affect me two decades from now?

When I was down in California, I went through the phase of conning everyone for everything I could. But you can only do that, you can only butt your head against the wall so many times before you realize, hey that hurts, what the fuck am I doing this for? And if you learn from that, you recognize it when it comes your way. It's not a matter of being hip, it's just a matter of being realistic. When somebody comes at you with a game, you just say, I don't have time for that, please take that elsewhere. And you can say it in such a way that the individual won't be insulted.

That's basically where I'm at right now. I've done it and, at that particular point in time, that was okay. It was something I had to learn. But you get to the point where you realize that no, you don't have time for that nonsense. It's a serious drain on the old brain. There are better things to do with your time than to go out and see what you can get from somebody else. Just do it yourself. You don't have to rely on anybody else.

That's another thing. In the past I've always relied on other people and when I came to the realization that I was going to be doing life-25, I had to rely on myself. Me and my mother sat down during PFVs [private family visits] and talked, and we've discussed the fact that she might not live until the end of my bit. That has had as much impact on me as getting life-25. She's fifty-two. So I've still got nineteen years left. My grandmother died when she was sixty-one. My grandfather, at seventy-five, just got remarried, so I mean, we've got good genetics in my family.

My father? He left when I was one year old. I don't even know his name. My mom remarried. She waited twenty-five years, until she remarried in June of '86, I believe. No, '85 I think. Yeah, it's that sort of thing; you lose track of years, and sets of years. They don't really have any bearing. It's difficult for me to remember back five years, ten years, because I have to look ahead.

I've seen some of my files. They won't release all of them to me, eh. I think basically they see that I'm dealing well with my time, because that's got to be obvious, because I haven't ... I have only received one charge in the last six years and that was just a little bit of hash in my house. And if you happen to occasionally smoke, that's natural, because you're bound to fuck up sooner or later. Other than that I've got nothing but excellent work reports from my supervisors. I've always done the best job that I could. I've tried to stay away from all the nonsense, so I think the overall picture is that we have an individual who's only got six years in on his life bit, but who seems to be approaching it responsibly and seems to be thinking about the future. And I think if you compare that attitude or that picture with the last time I was doing time ... the last time I didn't really give a fuck what was happening with the future. I had no direction and now the only way that I can get through the bit, the only way that I can survive it mentally, and maintain my personality, is to deal with it.

The average work day? I've got the job over there as the works clerk in the Works and Maintenance trailer. So, I basically make sure all the maintenance work orders are issued on time, and keep track of the funds that are spent on the various projects. Once I get their work out of the way, then there are two programs on the computer that I currently use; one is, of course, a game, which is just a release for me, and the other one is a [Microsoft] Works tutorial program that teaches you how to use spreadsheets and the various functions of the word processor. It's a good program to learn. It's quite a sophisticated setup. After work I go home, check my mail, have a coffee and, if there's nothing pressing on the television, then I go down to the hobby shop. I like to work with wood.

I'm also working in the canteen as the assistant manager there. Most paydays about sixty dollars of my pay, which is almost all of it, eh, goes into the dairy. I don't bother going to the canteen because I can get everything I need from the lifers store. So I just go in there, assign my sixty dollars and that's what I have to spend. It's called the dairy because our basic products are the coffee, the sugar, and the cream; and then we have our dairy products, which ranges from popsicles to tubs, malts, milks, the whole nine yards. We don't get any of those dairy products on the [food] line, except small vanilla cups and other things that it's not worth the effort to go down for.

I don't know, it's difficult for me to try to formulate a program that would deal with my needs, or the needs of other people doing a long amount of time, because I'm really not sure myself what it is that I would be able to get involved with. It would have to be something that would allow you to interact with males and females on things that happen in the community. It's difficult for me to explain.

One good example, we were talking once about how do you deal with no women. I am losing the ability to communicate with a female. I sit down with a woman guard, say, like Joan over in the hobby shop. She's the liaison for the lifers group. I find it difficult just to sit down and have any kind of conversation because I have no point of reference. I have nothing that I can really say to this woman, short of a game, and I'm not into the games. Like I've said, I've gone past that. I don't know.

The M-2 [Man-to-Man], that program there? That really doesn't do me any good. That's why I haven't gotten involved with it. Because if you have an individual who comes in to keep you company, to talk to you … talk to you about what? And what is the goal there? It's going to be nineteen years left. There's really nothing I can say to someone like that. So I'm losing my communication skills.

The life skills program that they have available, as I explained to my case manager, she wanted me to take life skills – why? The life skills program is going to change ten times between now and the time I get out, if ever. If I take it now, it's going to be irrelevant nineteen years from now. It's just not going to exist. Everything will change.

There has to be, I don't know, something that'll give an individual doing book a reason for going on. If you look at the way CSC is set up now, there is not one anywhere in Canada, in the federal system or the provincial system, a program set for an individual doing life-25. They don't exist. So with me right now, the only reason for going on is me.

I want to finish the time, get out and live the rest of my life in comparative peace and quiet. I don't know, I want to be prepared so that when I get out I can approach the parole board and say this is my plan, it's up to me. These are the skills that I have, this is the job that I want to do, this is why I want to do this, you know? All I can really do is just take it a day at a time, work towards my own personal goals, so that if I am ever given the opportunity to get out of here, then I'll be prepared.

I don't know, I can't think of a program ... social interaction, being aware of what's happening out in the community, being aware of the things that are changing in the world, and as long as I can stay in tune with what's happening and stay up to date ... I can't allow myself to stagnate, and that's one of the things that's happening here. If you isolate yourself too much you lose contact and when you get out there it's almost impossible to reintegrate yourself back into society. If I can somehow maintain contact, and right now the only way I can do that is through the TV (like I watch a lot of news and a lot of the educational programs) and I try to stay up on that, but that's a cold, very unrealistic ... like it's there; it's like food that you have to eat. It doesn't have to be good, but you have to eat it. I don't know, but I think that as time goes by, I'm slowly going to lose my communication skills. I'm going to be losing the ability to interact.

One of the ways that I've worked on to change that is I've kept myself extremely busy in here. Like I have my job over there; I'm the assistant manager in the lifers store; I'm the chairman of the lifers group. That forces me to interact, whether it's with other lifers, my superiors, my boss, acquaintances that I know. It helps me exercise that portion that wouldn't normally be exercised. And it helps maintain sanity. It may sound odd, but that's difficult, and one way to stay sane here in the Twilight Zone and doing as long as you're doing is look for the humour. If I can find something humorous every day, if there's something that I can look at and laugh at and realize I still have the ability to laugh, then I'm okay. So, I always look for the humorous.

UPDATE

Since his last interview, Burr has been transferred three times. The first move was to Matsqui's punitive segregation unit ("the hole"): "I got into a hassle with a couple of other guys. I was there for two and a half months when the IPSO [Internal Preventative Security Officer] grilled me every day for the names of the other guys. Basically, I was given the option of either giving up their names or being shipped to Kent. So I went to Kent."

After four relatively quiet months in Kent, he was transferred to the Regional Psychiatric Centre, where this interview took place. "This is the Twilight Zone. The rules are different from other institutions. If you are unable to laugh at it, it will grind you underfoot. You have to become stronger inside." His hope was to take the violent offenders program while at RPC, but that was not to be; he was ineligible to take the program because he had a diagnosed mental illness.

That mental illness was the reason the administration approved the transfer. He took the summit program for schizophrenics – a program he "passed with flying colours:" "I'm not schizophrenic. Even the psy-

chologist here says I'm not. Basically what happened was that I was misdiagnosed when I was nine or ten years old and the 'bug jacket' just followed me. And because it was easier for me, I didn't enlighten anyone. It was easy time on the psych ward [in Vacaville Prison in California]. Now I'm on what they call provisional status. They say I have an antisocial personality disorder – basically because I'm not actively participating in the normal institutional politics. But I'm not into that. I do my own thing. I'm not interested in that bullshit."

The best part of his stay at RPC, according to Burr, had been the gradual reduction in his daily doses of "bug juice", which he now likened to "a ball and chain wrapped around my brain. Nobody really knows who I am. Neither do I." The dosage was now down to twenty-five milligrams per day. By the end of the following week he expected to be off drugs completely. "It's given me a new set of eyes. I'm becoming conscious again. For the first time in my life, I'm looking forward to the future."

Burr's next step was to take the violent offenders program, some time in the next year or so. He said there was up to a two-year wait to get into the program – time he would most likely spend in a medium-security prison.

'If you don't do nothing, you get nothing.'

Ed was twenty-four when sentenced to life-25. He had served six years at the time of his interview.

I'm in my sixth year now. I was arrested January 1, 1985 and spent time at pre-trial at Oakalla, and then here at Kent. I've spent a short time in other institutions on separate charges. I started out with two years, escaped, went to Alberta, got another year added on to the two, got out on mandatory, got picked up on a rubber charge [writing bad cheques], got another two and a half years, which made five and a half years. The other joints I've been in have been in a population setting, so I basically had movement through the whole institution. There were PCs in Matsqui when I was there, but it was one little tiny unit, and they didn't fill them.

At Kent, about seven or eight got writs in right now on the double-bunking issue. It's all been denied so far. They're always reverting back to the fact that they delegated the PC population into Kent Max as only a temporary measure, and I mean it's been temporary for six years now.

I go to school as much as I can. I have another job in this unit, so

I manage to keep pretty busy. I spend a lot of time with myself, reading, writing. There are forty-eight guys in this unit, with a small yard that we can utilize. You got a situation like G-Unit, where they've got no yard time because somebody used a bar to try to pry the back gate open, so they took it away from them. And that's another situation where one guy screws up for everybody, right. Forty-eight guys over there now, and on a day like yesterday, population had their cells searched yesterday, and we didn't get a yard or programs corridor, so they were locked up in that hot unit all day, you know. There's always a certain degree of tension, even in population, right. But it's higher here because you've got more guys in here and they're all double-bunked, population at least they're spread out within six units. If you don't want to see somebody, you don't have to. Basically, you can ignore some person you don't want to see, and get away with it whereas in here, if you were in here and I didn't like you, and you lived in my unit, I'm forced to live with you, right? And wherever you go, you're going to see me and wherever I go, I'm going to see you. It just elevates the tension.

Still, it's easier to manage in some ways in PC because you can't get any lower on the ladder, right. You're at the bottom. The only place you can go is up from there and some people can go up, some people can't. Some people are stuck here, and there's nothing they can do about it. I'm not saying they're stuck in this institution, but they're stuck in a PC setting, right. There are some people that will be able to integrate out into a population. I think I could integrate into a population setting. What I see happening to me next is, I just beat one appeal, I should have another decision on my other appeal by September. The transfer coordinator here has a transfer package in on me; it's on hold, but it's in on me for Mountain. I just want to get out of here. I told them I wanted to make school my main priority. And, I can't do that in RPC. RPC wants to see me; they want me to do a program at RPC and I've already agreed that I'll take their violent offenders program.

Basically, the way it runs down is that if you come here and you've got a seven-year, nine-year, twelve-year sentence, you've got a better chance of getting out of here than if you come in here doing life. Especially life-25. I've seen a couple of cases where people that were doing life sentences, but with no date for parole eligibility set upon them, they left here in two years. Whereas every lifer that's doing a life-25 sentence that I've seen come into here, the only place they've left to go is RPC. And when they're finished their program at RPC, whether they completed it or whether they screwed up, they always came back here first, before they went anywhere else.

I dropped out in Grade 8. I upgraded that to Grade 10 equivalency while I was in jail. Once I got out of jail, I re-entered high school on the elevated program, where you jumped from Grade 10 to your Grade 12 in eighteen months – instead of the two years that it normally took. I got my Grade 12. I think the main reason I really pushed my schooling is because when I was out, when I was younger and out on the street, I didn't want to go to school. I would have preferred to have a job, and work or do whatever I was doing. But once I got into the jail setting, I was pretty well stuck there and I could attend school.

I still keep in contact with my family; whereas when I was in Drumheller, they were coming to visit me, here it would take, like, eighteen hours for them to come down for a visit … what, a three-hour visit? They've got the family visiting program here. I've approached my mom on it: it doesn't matter to me if my stepdad comes or not: I've approached my mom, and she's hummed and hawed. I was married; I'm divorced now, which took place after my incarceration. I've got one kid. Eight now. Boy. My parents have my child. The child that I have was not from my wife, it's from a previous engagement with another woman. All I have with my son is letter contact, that's it. I get, every Christmas, a card and a little letter with it, but, basically, that's about it. I get pictures.

Now we slip into my home life. My stepdad was rather violent, to put it mildly. He used to beat me up all the time. When my real dad split from my mother, there were three kids, me and my two sisters, one older, one younger. Now my dad wanted to take me because I was the only boy, right. And he said to my mom, you take the girls, I'll take him. And my mom said no … you take them all or you don't take any of them. Now, he didn't feel he was able to raise all three of us at that time, so he didn't take any of us. But over the years, the first five years after they split, he was always in contact. He lives in Portland. He knows I'm here. I contacted him when I was in Oakalla, and told him what was happening, and he went so far as to offer me a lawyer if I needed one. I've always had a good writing relationship with him – whenever I see him, there's never any problem – but I don't see him as often as I'd like to. It wasn't very much fun running away from home by yourself, so I always incorporated one of my friends to go with me. There was a lot of mothers out running around telling their sons, stop playing with him! But, I ran away a few times, got a six-month sentence in Centre Creek out here in Chilliwack and then settled down for a while. On my sixteenth birthday, I got my two-year sentence for break and enter and, when they sent me to Oakalla, Oakalla said no, they're not going to take him; send him to Stave Lake. So, en route to Stave Lake, I escaped and scored lucky, actually. A guy helped me out right from there, took me to his house; I was handcuffed, and everything. He got the cuffs off for me, and the next morning bought me a bus ticket, and gave me some money, got me all the way back to Cranbrook where I got my sister to hit the bank, and I went off to Alberta. When I got out there, I had some friends who were going to take me down into the States. They had a little van and they were going to whip me across the border and I missed them by half an hour. So, I started hitchhiking back and these two kids picked me up in a stolen truck; they were drinking and we got to Red Deer and we got pulled over for a routine check and we all got pinched. I knew I was going back to jail anyway because of the two year sentence, right? So I told these two kids, I said, look, I'll ride the beef on the truck and you guys can walk. So I got a year consecutive for that truck and then that put me in Drumheller. Once I got to Drumheller, the first federal institution I'd ever been to, I had a few problems when I first started out. The local tough guys in the joint trying to prove their way and basically I toughed it out, right, and it's not like now, where I'm doing a life sentence and a woman was killed in my crime. Okay, now if I go into a population setting, anybody that knows about that turns around and tells somebody else – they're going to put whatever they want into their scenario of what happened in the crime, and I'm going to have constant altercations all the time. So I turned around, and I said, I don't want to deal with it, I'll just come into PC.

This whole story reverts to when I was a juvenile. I was running away a lot, most of the time I was living on the street, so I became like a street kid. I was in a small town, but it didn't matter, I was still basically living on the street. So I run into this guy and started selling drugs for him. Well, after I got out of Elbow Lake at the end of this five-and-a-half-year sentence, I ran into this guy again in the bar and he approached me as a money partner, first of all, in a cocaine deal that he had going. So, I turned around and took together $10,000 in cash, and bought into this business. A friend of mine that I had hung around with when I was a kid, I turned around and approached him, and said, hey, if you can get this amount of money together, I can start making money for you too. So he went and talked to this girl he was living with. Her father had a lot of money, so he went to her, and she went to her father and he ended up getting the money. They were both in as money partners. He was a business individual in the community; he never even touched the drugs. One night he was at this party and there was a girl there. I don't know whether she was just trying to get ahead, or whether she was just trying to manipulate things so that she could get a free supply of drugs or whatever. But after the party the next day, she tried to work us into giving her some type of deal. We turned around and told her, like forget it, right ... okay ... and then she started following us and she found out where the main supplier was that we were getting it from; this business man. Well, she made the mistake of going up to the door, and basically putting it right on him in front of his wife and his kids. She demanded that she wanted some dope, or else she was going to go to the authorities. I was in the bar at this time and he came down, threw me up against the wall, stuck a knife up against my chest. I thought he was going to stab me to death right there in the bar. Finally we went out to the alley and talked it over, and while he's telling me what's happening, I put together that this is the same woman from the night before that had come onto us.

So about a week later, we got called out, and some guy told us that she was at this party, so we went down to this party, and during the course of the evening he tried to pick her up and take her out, and she wouldn't have anything to do with him. We waited until she left the party and picked her up on the street in the car, took her out to this gravel pit, and when we got to the gravel pit, all the way up to the gravel pit, he was in the back seat with her. I told him prior to all this that I didn't care what happened, but I was sitting in the car, I was having no part of it.

When he got her up to the gravel pit, he took her outside and he was beating her up, and I figured, well, that was the extent of it. She was going to get beat up and it would be over, right. I snorted some cocaine, so I'm sitting there listening to the radio, and the car I was in had the trunk button inside the cubby hole, right, all the windows were down, right, and I had my guns in the trunk of the car, my hunting rifles. So, I was sitting there and I saw his hand come through the window, open the cubby hole and push the trunk button, and I thought, well, now he's going to work her over with a tire iron, or something, like he might break her legs or something, but I didn't think at that point that it was going to turn into a killing. I opened the door and jumped out, and because we were in a gravel pit I slipped and fell on the gravel. Got up and went scrambling around the back of the car, and just as I come around the back of the trunk, he was standing over top of her, and I was just coming round the corner, and, boom … he shot her, and it was over at that time. She was lying there, dead.

I started shaking, and he ended up throwing me up against the side of my car and telling me to calm down. I was telling him, I'm getting out of here, I'm leaving you here, you can walk back to town, I don't care. He cuffed me around a little bit and told me to calm down. Finally, I calmed down and he told me, well, look, we'll take her out of here and we'll bury her and no one will ever know. I told him: well, I ain't touching her, right, you go ahead, you're doing it. I stood there and he dragged her off in the bush. Ultimately what I found out happened was all he did was break a whole bunch of branches down off a tree and cover over top of her, because he had designs on going back there the next day. I turned around and drove him home, and went home myself and fell asleep. My dad got me up the next morning, and we went to work. Months later, what happened is that he gets picked up for possession of cocaine. While they're talking to him, my name comes up. He tells them that he got the cocaine from me. The next day, the police come, storm my house, grab me, take me down to the police station.

There was no preliminary hearing. I was directly indicted and I got fifteen years. Now, I knew what the play was there, the Crown just wanted me in jail because there was a good chance that I was going to be at this murder charge. Right, so they wanted me out of the way. At my preliminary hearing, my co-accused, supposedly, is there. And he said something during his testimony, during the preliminary hearing, that made the police look at him for the first time. So, they went to arrest him, and he was packing his bags, getting ready to split. Now, they didn't have any evidence at this time; all they had was this body. So both of us were saying, no, forget it, right.

Okay, now because they wouldn't give us co-accused meetings, the Crown was going into him saying, hey, he's talking, he's talking, he's saying that you did it, and the Crown's coming to me and saying, hey he's talking, he's saying that you did it, right. And it didn't really work on me, but it was working on him. So, finally, he talked to his lawyer, and told his lawyer where a whole bunch of the evidence was, and everything else, and basically made this deal with the Crown. After he testified, I mentioned something to him. I was sitting there, and he had just been excused and I said something like, your tail fell out, or something, and he ran out of the courtroom and everybody started laughing, and the judge adjourned it for ten minutes to calm everyone down. So they took us out, they locked me in the room; well, I went right to the window that was pointing at him. And I told him, go downstairs to the back window – because it was open and I could talk to him, he was a story down, right. Okay, so he went downstairs and I started asking him, look, what are you doing, you're just digging a hole for yourself. And he turned around and yelled up into the window that if I sent anybody after him, he was going to kill my wife. Well, they walked out and two hours came back with a guilty verdict. We had already applied for a mistrial.

When the jury went out I thought, well, like basically what it turned around to was my story against his story. My word against his. And, I thought well, okay, there's a chance. I can remember my immediate reaction: I stood up, turned around and told my wife to file for a divorce. Now, up until this point, we had been in constant letter contact in Oakalla. I was writing her two or three times a week. The judge said ... how did he put it ... he says, well, there seems to be more criminal elements here than have been brought out by the court. He says, unfortunately – those are the words, the word he used was unfortunately – he says, unfortunately, you've been convicted of this by the jury and, I must pass sentence on you. He says: you've been convicted of first-degree murder, and the least sentence I can impose upon you is twenty-five years. That's when I stood up, turned around and told my wife, she was bawling, and I said, look, file for a divorce. And I was bitter, right. I mean, who wouldn't be. So, I told her to file for a divorce and she jumped up and across the gateway thing there, was hugging me and, no, no, she said, I'll never file for a divorce. And I told her, I said, wait five years, and you'll be happy to file for a divorce. And five years passed, and she still never filed for a divorce. And, finally I got hold of my lawyer, and I said, Look, find out what she wants to do. Now, the way I look at it is, I don't want to ruin her life. If it turns out that I go through six years of waiting for an appeal or whatever, and the appeal finally goes through and I win, well, then, who knows. I mean you can always get remarried. I didn't want to have her start up another relationship with someone else there, and having to worry about being married to me.

How would I characterize myself? Well, one way or another, this has changed me quite a bit. I'm at a point now where I've looked at age, at my age quite a bit lately. I'm thirty, I've got nine more to wait for the fifteen and they might give me eligibility, they might not. Okay, so I'll be thirty-nine then. If they don't give me the eligibility to apply, I'll be forty-nine by the time I get a chance to apply. I'll be fifty years old. That's a long time to spend in jail, and, for most people, prime years that they're putting their life together so that at fifty they can start looking back and saying: hey, I can kick back in ten years and I've got my house and I've got this, and I've got a family, and my kids, and blah, blah, blah. My kid's eight years old already. I've got a picture of him, standing on ice in hockey gear, playing hockey – and I've never seen him even skate. So that's what I'm looking at right now. Basically, I'm doing whatever I can, right now, to prove to the parole board when my time comes that I should have a chance. I'm not saying it's a right, because the parole board doesn't view it as a right. But what I'm doing is I'm doing my best to show them that I'm a big candidate for parole.

You could turn around and walk around in here like a vegetable, like some of these people do. There's some people in here that even go so far as to refuse to work, and mooch off everybody else. Now, I've chosen not to do that. I've chosen to try and keep myself paced with the outside as much as I can, and learn as much as I can, to change myself, basically. In a sense, having this happen to me, has helped me. If I hadn't got arrested, I would have got myself involved in that drug trade, right. Whereas this murder happened, and I got convicted and I got sentenced to jail. I'm here now, and now I'm looking at different avenues. My being here is superior to that person that I would have been then, in the sense that here I'm a criminal serving time, there I would have been a criminal doing crime.

Since I've started SFU, I've really thought of getting a BA in psychology, or even criminology. I'm a little leery about branching out into the criminology, but I'm going to take a couple of courses, and see what it does for me. I don't want to close any options to myself right now. I want to keep them as open as I can, and who knows. Basically what I'd like to see happen here now, because everything is so high-tech and computer out there, I'd like to see some computer courses coming to here. Now, if the age is high-tech now, with computer, look where it's going to be in 1999. If a person is going to leave this setting with what he came in here with, there's only one road to travel and that's right back into the environment that he left.

I never committed this crime; I was involved, but I'm not the one who pulled the trigger. For me to go and successfully begin taking this program, I've got to admit to my crime … which is one of the main problems. Basically what I'm looking at now is I'm going to have to turn around and go there and stand up in front of everybody and say, hey, I did this. And, not only lie to them, but lie to myself. Now, this is not something that I want to do, but this is something that I might have to do to take that program. If you don't take that program, basically when your eligibility comes up for parole, they turn around and they say to you, well, we've got you listed as a violent offender, and you've enlisted into the violent offenders program four times and yet you wouldn't admit to it; you've always dropped out. And they're not going to look at the reason why you dropped out, they're just going to look at the fact that, hey, you dropped out of that program. The only way I can break the logjam is I can apply myself in that direction and follow their road and say I did it, and sort of smooth the way to other programs, RPC, and ultimately another institution. I'm not saying that I'm not guilty, because I was there. I knew that something was going to happen; I didn't know it was going to escalate to the point that it did. But I was still involved, and even if the person was only going to get beat up, I was still going along with that.

If I don't beat this appeal, what I'm looking at is I got ten in by then, on the fifteen. Well, I'm just going to continue on … I won't reapply for an appeal. I mean it's, what, going to take another seven years until that? I can go through this whole twenty-five-year sentence in the appeal process, and not get anywhere. I'd rather turn around and make attempts at bettering myself, and turning around and proving to these people, whether they believe I'm guilty or not, turning around and proving to them that, when I get out, they don't have to worry about whether I'm guilty or not, because they're not going to have to worry about me reoffending. I've been in the system for a few years now, and I don't want to spend the rest of my life in here. All I can do, all anybody can do is make the best of what's available to you, and ultimately out of that, hopefully, each individual will get some direction to follow and pursue that direction.

UPDATE

The follow-up interview with Ed took place at Kent in the summer of 1994. He had just returned to Kent after completing the RPC program. He had been in "the hole" and only been out for a week (not for punitive segregation but because he was waiting for clearance for Mountain Institution). There were, however, allegations, which he vehemently denied, about his fiancée bringing drugs into RPC. He felt that he was being "victimized" by the current political context: the Greg Williams case at Kent (the highly publicized death of Williams's wife due to a drug overdose during a PFV), and the situation at Ferndale where two inmates had escaped from the minimum-security prison and had committed murder before being recaptured. As a result, he said, "staff were afraid to put a signature on a transfer warrant" and staff were also very leery about relationships between prisoners and women they had met through a "pen pal" type of correspondence (which was how he had met his fiancée). He commented that this was "the way the story goes."

The eight-month RPC program had been a "great help" to him; he had been able "to admit his guilt." At first others (those in his group and staff as well) had thought him "cold," that he "closed people off." During empathy and role-playing sessions, he had played his father and "broke down" – "laid myself out on the table, but the others did not pick at me." For him, the most dramatic aspect of the program involved writing a letter from the victim to himself, and also involved a partner playing the role of the victim's friend. Ed said that he would "never lose that letter."

He now realized, after RPC, that drug use had led him into his present situation. He now planned to work towards lower-security institutions and the fifteen-year judicial review: "if you don't do nothing, you get nothing." His relationship with his fiancée was of paramount concern, but his "eyes were opened now" – even if she left he could still go on and "not crawl into a shell." He had been free of drugs for several months before he had met her and would continue to be drug-free. At his first visit with her he had "told her the truth," that he was in for first-degree murder of a young woman.

LARRY

'I'm running out of time.'

*Larry was forty-six when sentenced to life-
25. He had served six years at the time of
the interview.*

Mission Institution is quite a contrast to Kent. I've only been in the holding penitentiaries, like Wilkinson Road, and maximum-security, Kent. Mission is much more relaxed, much more freedom. Activity-wise, there's no comparison with any of the other places, the other places were limited to almost no activity compared to here. I'm chairman of AA. I'm involved, of course, with the chapel group like I was at Kent. I'm involved with my school work. I have a job in Inmate Employment here that takes up my days. Hobby-wise, I've started glass work, stained-glass, and I've also kept up with my program exercise, and that type of thing. My BA degree could be finished next semester.

Quite a contrast to my life in the street, where I lost interest mainly. I was too involved in sports and whatnot to have any time to do school work. By the time I was fourteen, I was occupied with getting involved with the different programs and the sporting activities. I just didn't have time for homework. And I joined the army right out of high school.

Only what I read in books was what I knew about prison. James Cagney, etcetera. That was my first big disappointment, it wasn't like I pictured it! You know, like in the old films of the thirties and forties, with the tiers, and the rows of cells, and it was quite different. From what I observed since I've been in, there's different types of people in these places, and there's some that have spent their whole lives in prison. And they usually wind up coming back when they get out and then there's others, it's just a one-time thing, and I've noticed quite a few that I think will progress somewhere, eventually, even guys doing a life-25 that will probably get out at the first judicial review just by their record. And I optimistically look at that angle, that fifteen years, 1999 is when I become eligible. I was convicted in '84. Only thing, I'm running out of time. When the offence happened in 1984, I was forty-six, so I'm just now coming this month to my fifty-third birthday. Well, the old age pension comes at sixty-five, so I'll have a nice little nest egg for when I get out. I plan that I'll probably be here for a few years, and that'll take me almost through to ten years into my sentence and then there'll be five years to fill in somewhere – either next door to here at Ferndale, or at William Head, or possibly Elbow Lake, I guess. But in that time, I plan to continue on as I am, taking whatever suitable courses I can and getting involved in various hobbies. And there's a lot of groups that come in, and as you move down in security, you get more and more of these coming in. It's been quite an eye-opener for me to come into a situation where I have all this spare time, because I never seemed to have enough before. Now I have an abundance, and I'm just doing things that I never had any opportunity to do before, which includes my school work. All my life I've felt badly about not going to university and getting some sort of a degree. And I used to chum around with a lot of guys who graduated from McGill and U of T and I always envied those people, but I knew I just wouldn't have enough time ever in my busy life to dedicate that much time – so it's been a godsend that way.

Another thing I'd like to mention: I've always, all my life, wanted to read certain books, and never had the time. I read *Gulag Archipelago* way back, and my wife thought I was nuts reading that stuff. That's the kind of thing I've always liked reading and just never had enough time to read. But now I have the opportunity and the time, and then getting into my BA in history, it just opens everything up.

The only shock I ever got that I remember was on my initial arrival at Kent Institution. I'd only been there for a very few days, and I received a piece of mail, institutional mail, whatever it's called, and on there it had that I'm eligible for day passes or unescorted, or whatever, escorted I guess it was, passes, temporary absences, in the year 2006. And that kind of made me open my eyes, and, of course, my full time was up in 2009. So, three years prior to that I qualified for temporary absences from the prison. That was the only thing that kind of shocked me. I thought it was very ignorant of them to send me something like that so fast. I thought they could have waited a few years. I spent time in the military before, and you had to go twenty years to get a pension, so I just used that context when I finally adjusted myself to the fact. I figured, you know, I'd have to qualify for another pension before I got out, which would be the old age this time, so I just kind of used it that way. And then I forget about it because I remember how fast time can go. When I first joined the air force, I was very young, and I remember joining and I thought to myself: some day I'll be retiring, whether it's three years, ten years, twenty years and I'll look back to this day, and think, boy, that went by fast! And the next thing I knew I was in my mid thirties and I was looking back and thinking, wow, did that ever go fast, and I know it'll be the same situation here, although at the start it looks impossible. Once you're into it, and especially at times like this, when I've just moved down from a place like Kent that I was used to, and doing time at, and was getting along fine and managing my time well and wasn't having any problem – then to get to a place like this. It's … it's just so much nicer here and it's such a better environment except, you know, there's certain areas that are bad, but overall it's quite an improvement. Now, I'm not too sure whether I want to go over there, to Ferndale, because there you will have guys coming and going every day to their jobs and going downtown with passes, etcetera. I don't know if I'd really like to be in that situation. I know I wouldn't want to be there for a couple of years anyway.

I deserved to be in prison. I wasn't innocent of my crime. I felt really sorry for anybody that was in a prison wrongly convicted. At least I was there, you know, the right way. I knew I was guilty. I thought they were kind of harsh on the first-degree thing. I figured, a lovers' quarrel and crime of passion was never going to go beyond the second-degree level, but the way I've done it, with my drinking and everything, I guess I didn't leave the authorities too many options but to push for first-degree, although everything that happened was done through drinking, there was nothing in a sober mind that was planned. I kind of expected I would get convicted of second-degree murder because it was a crime of passion. It was so unbelievable, from the onset. I was in the hospital; I had injured myself and was under medication when the Justice of the Peace came in and read me the charges for murder, and I asked the cop who was in the room with me who I'd killed. I was in a fog from the start, and it was like that for quite a few months afterwards. I tried to piece it all together, although I knew that I'd done it – because it was obvious – it was just that the memory wasn't there. I had a definite history of blackouts from my drinking, and there was no notice taken of that fact by anyone in the courts, or the police or anyone involved in the trial. What I've seen throughout the whole thing is that for those in the know in the prisons it is very simple to get around the problems that I had, and it's only the innocent and the ones who have never been in prison – the guys in here called the Straight Johns, they're the only ones are going to get the twenty-five, life-25. You know, we sit around the hotels and drink and play the part and everything, but we're not, you know, prison-wise, so when we do make a mistake, it's usually a huge one, and we pay for it, because we're not sophisticated in the ways of the courts, and the system that can give you a life sentence. There's lots of guys who have done the same thing as me and brag about it and they get manslaughter, five or six-year sentences.

Well, fortunately I had already met a few of the different guys that were in Kent, you know, in Wilkinson Road and whatnot, so I did have a few people that I knew. And the biggest bonus of all was to find when I got there that there was a school and some place where I could get away. I had no idea before I got to Kent that I'd have any freedom. I'd never been in these places – I didn't know what maximum-security was all about. I knew I'd be treated like a peon, but I wasn't too sure just how harsh it would be. And the only thing I'd hoped for before I got there was a little patch of grass somewhere that I could sit out on on a nice day, and it turns out there's a huge soccer field, ball field, so that was a huge bonus. And then when I found out that we had access to this thing for an hour or two a day, that was another huge bonus. So now I had my grass, a place to sit out on and maybe read a book, do something to pass the time, and then I find out there's this university there. I was just so flabbergasted with what was available, that it took away any of the harshness that I could have felt.

I find the guys doing the shorter sentences have the biggest problems and do the harder time. I'll give you one example … Brian. Here's a guy doing two years who's just completely ripped to pieces, doesn't know how to do each day! I think you resign yourself and you get along, as soon as you resign yourself to the fact that you're going to be there a while, and how you're going to do your time. Look around and see some old guy sitting in a bed smoking, and, you know, growing paler each day and you say, no, I don't want that. I use it as a challenge, I guess, to get through the whole thing and come out trying to look like a normal person.

There's lots of violence, no shortage of it. I just have my little run-ins with different guys, you know. They've turned out to be just flighty, they were after everybody, and, so, you know they don't get what they want out of you they'll just go on to the next guy. I just didn't pay them attention actually, and that worked fine, and like I said, I was lucky enough to know a few guys that were, you know, looked up to in the institution. And they knew me, and I guess put in a good word in for me somewhere because I just haven't had that problem.

I didn't drink for almost four years before this thing happened with me, and then it was just after one day. Once I'd come to the realization of what had happened and the time I had to spend, then I could have said, well, that's fine, I'll just continue drinking, and do whatever, until. But I've never wanted to; I never wanted to before that, and I've never since I've been in prison ever taken a drink, or had a smoke of anything, or any pills, or whatever. They're all quite available.

I've had guys come up and shove things into my hands, and rather than make a big scene, I've just taken and dispensed with it somewhere. Every day I've done since I've been in prison has been without any chemical. There's lots of alcohol around. I used to laugh and watch the guys going to the AA groups and whatnot in jail, to impress the authorities, and then you'd see them drinking the home brews that were available. It's just a mockery. A lot of guys used to go to that group all the time, and of course when they get out on the street after, they just continue on.

There's plenty of humour. I've never had a shortage of laughs. There's a few drab people who never smile and never laugh, but I would say, you know, the majority do joke and kid around. There's no end of it. I just kill myself laughing at guys like Clyde. There's just lots of guys like that. And he went out, you know, he had forty days, just like Moses in the wilderness, out of Kent, and he came back, and he'd lost I don't know, forty or fifty pounds, I guess, and he got arrested stealing a side of beef out of a meat market. The forty days he was out, I think he was in forty fights.

When I got here, the only real conversation I had with anybody was the fact that they wanted to send me back to Kent. There was an East Indian guard. I was asking how I went about doing this, doing that, and he wouldn't give me any assistance, and I said, well, what are you guys here for? And he said: well, we can send you back to Kent. I've seen lots of the guards here who are quite friendly, and they will go out of their way if you do talk to them, but I haven't got to that point yet. I'm still getting used to the culture shock of Kent to here. And, you know, there's a few other little things that are still bothersome. I had PFVs at Kent all of the five years – I saw the kids – and since I've been here, they won't give them to me. They're not cleared. Kent didn't do their paperwork. So one of the penalties I've paid for coming down in security is that I've lost my PFVs, but eventually they'll be instituted.

That's the hardest part, to see humans sitting there day after day, following these weird orders that they have, and half of them don't even know the orders and they're just incompetent. And I always waited for one of them to say something to me at Kent, because I had a few choice words, you know, that I knew they wouldn't understand and, of course, I never did say anything and I never will, but I just have a hard time understanding anybody that would sit there and waste their life like they do. You know, they could do a lot of good. I guess some of them do, they pick one guy that they like and go to bat for him. I'm sure that must happen, but you don't see that much evidence of it. I just don't understand them. I was in the military, and I was in there for the sports because we had lots of trips, lots of drinking, and somewhat better job selection for me. But, when I finally got out and saw what I'd missed all those years in the business world – the access to the better wages, and the travel and the nicer things, you know, the new cars and that sort of thing, then I thought, man I was silly to have stayed so long. Now that I'm in here I still have my little pension that I get, and it gives me a bit of an edge. But it was just, when I got out of the military and thinking back all those years, really, I was something like these guys in here, sitting round doing nothing, collecting a paycheque. You know, in my case, it was playing sports and drinking; in their case, it's who else would give them a job, I guess. Half of them, anyway, it's hard to really deal with them. And you hear them, quite often, you'll hear them making a deal on this house or that house. I just sit there and I know the whole rigamarole involved because I was a realtor, and I feel sometimes like piping up because I heard a couple of times when I could have given them some good advice, but I had to bite the tongue on that.

My situation happened in 1984 and, about two days after the actual event, I was notified that I was charged with murder. Well, I asked the cop in the room, who died? And he told me, and that was the last thing that was ever done about it, until today, nothing has been done. There's never been anybody from the system, no psychologist, no psychiatrist, nobody, no unit manager, no case manager, nobody has ever talked to me about it until this interview. And I'm almost six years into my sentence. And the first thing I thought was, boy, I'm going to get bombarded with shrinks, and all kinds of questions asked now: what happened, what caused this and that. And nothing like that has happened. I noticed a lot of people after they commit a murder, they're sent for evaluation at Riverview, or whatever it is. I know a lot of guys in here are doing that, life sentences for murder, they all went through that thirty-day assessment period, but nothing like that was ever done in my case. I think that some attention could be paid to the guy's prior history: in my case, I don't think anything was done except for the fact that I killed this person and that I was guilty as sin, and it all pointed to first-degree, and that was the easiest thing to do. The prosecutor had a simple case … and the defence lawyer I had was incompetent and didn't do anything … so they had an easy conviction. Now, if they had looked at the fact that I had spent twenty years in the military – don't look at the fact that I was a drunk, don't look at the fact that I just played around – but I did give twenty years to the military. I had a stable work record all my life and was no problem, except for the odd one or two impaired charges. I thought that some attention could have been paid to those types of things, and it wasn't. Nothing was even thought of, and then of course the emotional and passionate side of things in my situation should have been, I thought, dealt with.

The onus is on me to do something, I guess, while I'm in here. In my mind the first thing I saw was the university, and I've done that, just completed that. Then, the time period being so great, do you start when you first come in, looking for rehabilitation or whatever they want to call it, or do you wait until you're further into your sentence? And I've seen judicial reviews, where the jury has paid attention to the fact that the guy started when he first came in to rehabilitate himself, and then another guy didn't do it until just a few years before the review, which is the best way to. If you do it just a few years before, then it's fresh in your mind, whereas if you do it when you first come in and then wait ten years you've forgotten it. Before you go to the judicial review, you go to the life skills, you talk to the psychologist, you get some sort of assessment done. So, when you go into the judicial review, you have all that done.

If I were trying to improve the system, I would get some people that are qualified, number one. What you get in here is what you get in the military, and you get it all the time, and a lot of people are just collecting a paycheque and doing nothing. And if someone wanted to try to help someone in here, they could, but they don't. Like I said, only on certain special occasions will they do it, I guess if somebody goes every day and talks to them, and wins their confidence, or whatever it takes to get them that way, then maybe they will get some help from somebody. But for the average guy who's got a little bit of pride, that's where I'm coming from. I just can't be bothered talking to someone sitting in a chair like that, day after day, doing nothing. And, what can they help me with anyway, and why would I bother? And I'm so far away in time, you know, you just get all these things running through your head. Why would I even want to talk to them? So it kind of gets to be a catch-22 here, damned if you do and damned if you don't. I mean, these people aren't that stupid that they can't figure out who the threats are and who the average guys. There's a lot of guys in prison, a lot of guys who won't reoffend ever again. That doesn't take a brilliant man to figure out who they are. What good does it do to leave a guy five years in Kent, like myself, when guys that are knowledgeable and can play the game can get out in three doing the same, or even less. I've known some guys get out in less than two years doing the same thing, because, you know, they snivel and whine. I don't know how you get around that, but I think there are definite areas for improvement. In this day of electronic monitoring and all that sort of thing, there's much more advantageous ways whereby both the government and the person being incarcerated can be doing the time. Well, I think that anybody who views these places and comes and gets involved and sees the expense, and who they're holding here and why they're holding them, and what it's costing them. I mean, it's just staggering, the amount of money that just this place here spends in a year. Kent's the same or worse. But you know, if the public was educated to that aspect, they would definitely demand that these twenty-five-year sentences get remodelled or something get done, even if it's capital punishment reinstated. There's so much waste in these places. I just can't even begin to guess across Canada what it's costing. All kinds of waste, every situation you can think of.

But there's another side to it, too. Take a look around here, at the mountains, the scenery and the area. I'd say about ninety percent or eighty percent of the guys in here could never afford to live in an area like this. And a lot of them, when they get out of these places, had a nicer deal in here. I had, you know, all these groups to go to, all these hobbies available, and all these nice meals, nice room and bed, and comfort – and I can just go back to that. How do I go back there? I just go and take a whole bunch of money out of the place, or steal a bunch of drugs or something. If I don't get caught, I'm okay; if I do get caught, I'm okay. So a lot of these guys use this for their home, and there's a lot of people living worse than in here. They're out there on the street right now. I'm telling you, this is a lot better than freedom to a lot of people. I mean, there are people that have freedom that don't live half as good as guys do in here.

I've got all sort of plans. I've purchased a couple of little places, so I'll have my own little farm or whatever it is. And I got a few people out there that I still keep in contact with. I have my kids and my family. So, I'll just have my little place out in the woods there, and I'll be a professional stained-glass maker by then, maybe write the odd little novel.

Before I just didn't have time to stop to see who I was or where I was going. Now, at least I've had a chance to put the brakes on because I was running out of control when this happened, as you can well imagine. I didn't know where I was going from day to day and that's the problem with it all. And, of course, my solution was, let's go get drunk and forget the whole thing, and that's exactly what I just about did, because I came within a fraction of dying that day. I tried to kill myself. If the police hadn't found me, I would have died. So, anyway, when I came to the realization of what had happened, and the fact that I'm still alive, and then all the good things that I still had access to, I pulled in my horns and stopped and thought about things. That put me on the right track. Life definitely has improved. And, I only see, for whatever time I have left here on this earth, it's going to be great; if I stay here for the rest of my time on earth, this isn't bad. It's fine, much better than Kent. Kent was much better than Wilkinson Road, so, you know, things have improved in that regard.

UPDATE

When Larry was interviewed at William Head in the summer of 1994, he was suffering from a self-confessed case of the "jitters": he had been running around all day getting things ready for his wedding the next day. He was "flabbergasted" at the conditions he'd found at William Head, "it was like at a wealthy retirement men's club", complete with ocean view. He'd arrived at William Head in 1993, after completing the RPC program and returning to Mission for two weeks before his transfer to Vancouver Island. The RPC program had helped, particularly to see things from the victim's position. Before RPC, no one had been interested in talking to him — except during our previous interviews. He'd met his fiancée at an AA roundup at Mission Institution, for which she had been one of the organizers.

Lifers were actively recruited at William Head, for they were a "stable group", a "good asset," in Administration's eyes. There had been lots of booze and drugs there and he was still involved with the AA group and chapel. He'd received his BA degree from SFU in 1991 at Mission (History major, English minor). He still ran eight miles a day and in two years would have reached his superannuation. When he got out, he'd like to help guys out from prison, perhaps working with the CSC in this regard. This "resort" was still a prison and there were still "mickey mouse rules and there's lots of them; but if you have to do time this is the place." He added, in conclusion, "Before I just didn't have time to see where I was or where I was going. Now things are still getting better; it's going to be great."

'Nothing is constant, except the drive to prove my innocence.'

Ken was eighteen when he was sentenced to life-25. He had served seven years at the time of the interview.

I'm not guilty. I've been in close to seven years and I'm still in an appeal process. I was accused of first-degree murder. Premeditated murder, which carries a term of life-25. It was a girl who had been murdered – it's hard to say murdered – who was found in a burned out fire pit. Apparently someone had tried to incinerate her body. I admitted to being the last person, that I knew of, to be with her. I was cooperating with the police up until the time they began to point fingers behind my back. In my eyes, they were trying to get me locked up, right? I wasn't going to play into their hands. I think that was when most of the trouble started, when I started not being so cooperative.

At the preliminary hearing, it was found that there wasn't sufficient evidence to bind me over to trial on first-degree murder. There was nothing, not even any proof of premeditation, so I was bound over on second-degree to stand trial. A month before my trial was due to begin on the second-degree murder charge, it was announced that I was now being indicted for first-degree murder on new evidence. This new evidence was an individual who was in remand around the same time as I.

The thing that bothered me most about this is the fact that I was blamed, firstly, with the death of a woman. And then to have this other clown, who was a rapist, saying that that was my motive. That's something that I've been dead set against ever since I was a kid, since I was able to form those ideas myself.

Anyway the odd thing about all of this is that he had given them their information, said to have come from me, prior to my preliminary hearing, and they never used it. And then the evidence he gave contradicted all the factual evidence of their experts, so it's really difficult to express how angry I am with that: that I could be raised up to first-degree murder without them having any factual evidence. So, on the basis of somebody who was obviously looking to make his own life easier, I was convicted of first-degree murder.

But at the time, you know, I didn't care that they had sentenced me to spend the rest of my life in jail because I was right. And what's right is what's right, you know? I'd done nothing wrong.

Yeah, it's been close to seven years, like I said. It seems I'm going to spend the rest of my life desperately counting on appeals and stuff. But in that way I knew what was going on. Even then I had no false impressions that everything was going to be speedy. I mean, in a matter of nine months, they'd managed to put me away for the rest of my life. So, I wasn't into this illusion that my lawyers were telling me. That, you know, appeal processes are quick and that I would be a free man again soon. I wasn't fooling myself by any means. I didn't know what to expect, but I figured I'd just take it one day at a time and see where it went, how it presented itself, and deal with it. In the mean time I wait. I have to take it one day at a time regardless of the amount of time that it takes. I ain't a rich man, so I have to be sort of patient with the system as it is. I mean, if it had been, like, ten years difference – that is, had this happened ten years in the future, and I had those ten years to work on something – perhaps I wouldn't be in the same situation, because of the financial aspect. I mean, at eighteen, you haven't got a whole lot, have you? And because I've been fiercely independent all my life, I don't ask that of my family, or, I guess, what people look upon as family.

Oh, it was a good home life. I stayed with my mother. I had two younger brothers. Three and five years younger. In that aspect, I was probably an only child. I could really expound on it, but I don't think there would be any clarity for you.

What does school conjure up in my mind? Well most of my life experiences were at that age anyhow. I went to Grade 7. I was thirteen. I look upon it as a sort of foundation to some things. Other things were of value. Isn't anything in particular I can remember. Not strong memories, or fond memories. Actually, I enjoyed school until I was in Grade 4. My parents were divorced at about that time, so there were a lot of other things that I wasn't sure of at the time and didn't know how to deal with. When I quit school, I was attending Grade 8 at the time. The transfer from elementary to high school was a little difficult. New situations sometimes affected me. I liked to be sure of what was going on about me before I'd get into anything. And then there was other mitigating circumstances that had me not attending school.

Well, up until the beginning of the high school year, I used to hang around an automotive shop, work on vehicles, high performance type, and the like. When I was about eight I helped tear apart the family car and put it back together. I guess I had a family influence there; my grandfather was a mechanic. I was just following – like a lot of guys.

And I had a friend whose father was an alcoholic and who was back and forth in foster homes. Nothing stable, eh. I'd known him since we were three years old. He left just at the beginning of grade school and I didn't see him again until I was thirteen. We got ourselves into some predicaments. Got involved with other people in the criminal context. Most of it centred on cars. I really like driving. I just kind of went along for the sport of it all at the time. You know, like, you have a friend and he's your friend, and you had to go with your friend.

Oh, I got caught for a good percentage. For a time I went to Youth Detention Training School – when I was fifteen until my seventeenth birthday. I escaped from there and got caught many times before finally settling down and looking at it properly. Because I really didn't know what I was doing, I didn't ask myself that question, what am I doing? I just went about doing things.

That's all changed now. Right now the only important thing is my appeal and I have to choose my steps very carefully so that I don't jeopardize anything like that. Some people see me as, you know, as a lifer and think, what has he got to lose? He's doing the rest of his life in jail. What I have to lose is a chance of being vindicated on this. But I think that if you keep yourself as busy as you can, then you stay out of trouble – depending on the personalities involved at the time.

When I walked in here, like, an old adage I picked up was, you came into this world alone, and you're going to go out alone. I've always been a person who stands on my own two feet, so I never looked for alliances to, you know, to lean on. That's not to say that I don't form friendships. It's just that they mean something different to me than just having someone around who'll back you up. I mean, if I'm not capable of doing that myself, I perish, right? You deal with what you're presented with. We deal every day with personality and mood changes. And you deal with them as best you can. Not everybody gets along, you know? Like, you have to keep yourself in check. Especially in this place because of the people.

If you look at all the different personalities, each person has a different personality, and there's always something in the character that has a ... I hate to use the word flaw. Perhaps our characters are flawed. I don't know. But you have to deal with that. I mean a lot of lifers live right here in K-Unit. A lot of people are doing a lot of time, and it fluctuates all the time. You get different people in here almost every day. There are some people you just don't step on, don't step on their toes, because you might not like the outcome, right? And that can get to be a scary situation in itself, being that there are so many insecure people here. You rely on the officers a lot as referees. They take on a little more authority, for instance, than a referee.

Here, in a confined environment like this, is probably the most stressful possible. But I kind of thrive on it. I've learned to thrive on it. I mean, if you're stuck in a spot where things need to be done, you deal with them – because you have to. I guess we all have built in endurance. You have to endure a certain amount of things. Once you accept them and know what they are and how to deal with them, I think that you can overcome anything. Basically, I just sit back and weigh the situation and figure out exactly what is happening.

But not everything that appears to be happening is the actual thing that is happening. There's an undertone to it that is in control, whispered, that you have to root out first. If you're able to root it out, you know, in your thought processes, from the different clues that are given, you know how to combat it. An approach I always look at is, and this probably comes from the first time I came in here, is don't trust anyone. I mean you can trust people to the limits as long as you know what the limits are, or you're going to lose. If you overstep yourself, get caught up in a situation where you're no longer in control, then you're going to lose. So you control a situation, or just allow the situation to run its course. I mean you have to deal with that on your own. And how you deal with it is going to affect how your tomorrow is.

Like I said, you have to be in combat mode at all times, you have to have your eye open for the manipulations that take place, because you're always in a vulnerable spot. Every waking moment you're in a vulnerable spot in here, and you have to somehow get the edge so that you're not so vulnerable. Sometimes you have to show that you care little about anything. And at other times, you have to show that you care a whole bunch. This is so that people don't get the misunderstanding, or the misconception that they think they should look out. You have to play a very fine line in here, because there's personalities who, you know, if you look at them sideways, they'll be leering around the doors for a week thinking you're mad at them. Or there's the type that have their own little trip.

A lot of people I have to describe as followers, and there are some who have devious minds and who feel that they might have a grudge against you for some reason or another, but they're not quite sure how to go about getting to you. They don't want a direct confrontation with you, so they go about trying to badmouth you to a degree, but not to the degree where you can say, like, you're in trouble now, right? More like, what the fuck is going on with you, you fucking dunderhead?

And they'll have others backing them up, and they'll all kibitz, eh. They're kibitzers and, you know, they think they know what's going on when they don't have a clue. So, you have to … I mean, it's a game in a sense. You have to weave it, you know, weave in there, and throw it all out of context for them so they really don't know what's going on. It gets to be funny after a while.

Sometimes things get a little confusing here too. I do the canteens, and ITFs [Internal Transfer of Funds]; you work with people's money. Well, it appears you're working with people's money, but all you're doing is shuffling paper. And I've had the job for over two years now and people still believe that I have a safe in my house that I pay them manually with. So when they ask about tapes, like do I have tapes for them? Sometimes I come up with a smart-ass or sarcastic answer to this for them. You know, sidetrack them for a couple of days until they get back to me. If it's really important they'll get back to me; if not, I just leave it.

Basically I'm not involved in a whole lot, just the daily routine around here. That's how I do most of my time. I try to keep everybody involved, you know? The biggest ally we have is the visits, social activities, when there's family involved and stuff like that. I do my best to try to keep that together and working properly. And I try to make sure that there are activities in here, that you have to keep happening, so that people don't become stagnant – and become violent.

I'm quite an independent person. I pick up on things and I do them merely to keep myself busy. I'll get into something and I'll watch it and see if it intrigues me or not. Sometimes I invent things to keep me busy. Most of the things take a couple of weeks anyhow. I usually have at least seven or eight things on the go all the time, so that if I ever do get to that point, there's always something else I can do to take that staleness away.

For instance, it's about a year since I've been here in K-Unit. I remember coming here and each gate to the tiers were locked and you had five-minute movements and this ridiculous thing of locking you up in your cell at eight-thirty at night on Tuesdays and Thursdays. This was happening in the summer, and when I came in here the people who were in here were – I don't know why – but they were satisfied with being ordered around. They didn't seem to have the ability to think for themselves or to conduct their own lives, because they're in prison. This is their prison, as I see it. It's my prison. I live here. A lot of things got dropped in here, and the people who were here at the time, you had to tell them, this isn't the way it's supposed to be, guys.

Seemed like the officers had a free rein in here. You're in a fishbowl in this place. I mean, the tensions of being confined are getting more and more all the time, you know? They made me tear down some privacy curtains I'd put up. I put them up because there's women working in here. They come and stop by your house and rip things down, you know, and then give the lame answer, well they're not regulation issue. I mean, you can't go to the washroom without being looked at. What kind of shit is that?

I go to an extreme at some points. You know, if you're going to, you know, if you start invading my territory, like this is my cell, don't you start prowling my cell. I've been crucified for the things that I did in here. I mean, I spent nearly three months in the hole at one stint because I didn't want them to look at my legal papers, right?

And you have them telling you how they think you're performing and all that on a regular basis. But I don't care what people say about me. I guess I don't because of my appeal. Everything relates around my appeal. To look at them, and to worry about what they think? They're two-faced. I mean, they're going to present things differently than they actually are – in their writing anyhow. Like, they'll jot things down, tidbits they hear and that, as actually happening.

So, I really don't care what they have to say about me because, hopefully, like I'm looking at it optimistically, none of that stuff will even matter anyhow. And if I'm not successful, I'm going to be forty-three anyhow, so the likelihood they'll be letting me out is …

I know that I'm doing life – the rest of my life, at present. But, like I say, hopefully it won't stay that way. And I'm optimistic that it won't. Perhaps that's what's keeping me going, that there is the chance that one day I'll be vindicated. But still, maybe because of it, I don't like to hear about others' short time. Like, I find myself associating with people who've done time. I guess they're a different kind of person.

Most of the people that are doing shorter time have different types of personalities. They don't look upon it as if they're living here. They're just doing time, a stint, you know? So, they really don't care too much how they live, or what goes on about them. It doesn't happen all that often, but some of them forget where they're at, you know? And you have to really pick and choose the times when you tell people where they're at, or you can find yourself in a whole lot of trouble, right? So, like, when you try to explain to somebody, most of the time as briefly as possible, that they are in prison and that their mouth is getting ahead of them, most of them realize what's going on and that perhaps they should keep themselves in check and figure out what it is they're doing that's bothering some people.

I don't look far into the future. When I do look into the future it's to do with my appeal. It has nothing to do with lower security, or more privileges, or anything like that, you know? They have me in prison. I'm not going to jump into a facade where I believe that, you know, this ain't such a bad place. I can do time here. Because I'm still doing life and nothing's changed. So whether it's here or in a lower security, I don't look upon being in lower security as being advantageous to me. I just don't see it – perhaps because I haven't looked at it. I mean others who have done time in a lower security are saying they want to go back there. Perhaps there is something there for them. To me, it doesn't matter where I do my time. I could do it in a cage because it's still time, and I'm not doing it for myself. They're doing it to me. Perhaps that's no way to look at it, but you have to.

Oh, there are certain things that I guess that I daydream about doing, you know, experiences I've had before. Any number of things. But I was only eighteen when I came in, for Christ's sake. I don't have a lot. ... When I get out? Oh, that's a very difficult question to ask of me being that I'm doing life. You know what I mean? Well, if you've got me this far – the way I look at it is, you know, any number of things could happen. Perhaps, say there is a judicial review in fifteen years and I'm successful in that, what will I do after that? I think that I'd have to plan that before I go up for this review. There's still at least eight more years to go. It's kind of a futile effort as I look at it. Well, most of the things are recreation type things, flying a plane, and going around in a boat, riding, gardening, that sort of stuff. Doing everything that everybody sort of associates with freedom.

Nothing in terms of a profession, no. That's something that I have considered, but it's too premature to do that. I would just be setting myself up for a downfall. I mean, to think that twenty-five years of your youth is gone. Ask people what formed those years. I mean, the years, right? I mean when I get out, I'm almost an old-age pensioner. What have I got? I ain't got fuck all. I haven't got any of the things that other people have worked towards. I've lost a lot of years, productive years, you know. From eighteen to forty-three, what the fuck do you want me to do? I mean, how can you even look at something like that? I mean, I've tried many times, and it's such a distant, distant question.

For the time being, I don't contemplate doing anything. Nothing is more pertinent in my mind than my appeal. Unless those avenues are finalized, unless those are all exhausted … I have another avenue which I intend to take if need be.

UPDATE

Ken was still pursuing his appeal, even though he had been unsuccessful in his applications to the BC Court of Appeal and to the Supreme Court. He was now applying to the Minister of Justice under Code 690, which can provide for a new trial if new evidence materializes. And new evidence had come forward: while at Kent Institution a prisoner told Ken that he had given false information to the informant whose testimony had proven crucial in his case. Ken was in good spirits and maintained that he had "never given up hope," that it was "the only thing" he had to go on with. He was now married and things were going well with his wife and her daughter from a previous relationship. He had met her at a

Christmas social at Kent in 1989 and they were married five years later. Life was "difficult" with PFVs only every two months. Nevertheless, things seemed to be working out. He had twelve years in now and, if all legal channels to prove his innocence were exhausted, he still had the judicial review at fifteen years to look forward to. In the mean time, he had "decided to get on with the sentence." One thing he had learned, "the void, there's no escaping it; everything is forever changing, nothing is constant except the drive to prove my innocence." His life would "never be as complete as dreamed about when a kid," but "you do what you have to do and as the story turns out I am doing well."

'Drugs for the public ... '

*Terry was twenty when he was sentenced
to life-25. He had served eight years at
the time of the interview.*

There's not much to do here. Like in a word – boring. And Kent's
the only place I know that's double-bunked, right? So, it's boring
and crowded.

The personal interaction with the people that are in here, what's
that old saying, familiarity breeds contempt, well I feel a lot of contempt, all day. It's like nobody cares. It's like this at Kent in particular. The interaction with the guards is usually on an anger basis. But
in a word, Kent is boring; just for a word.

It was different at RPC. There was always something to do there.
It was like, you know, you're in a program and that program is what
you do. You go from point A to point Z. You have your little side
programs such as working out, jogging, bringing up your school to
Grade 8, or whatever. There's paperwork every day. So you're
never really bored. You could get bored doing paperwork. But
there's something to do every day. There's no real major sitting
around like here. When I leave school I can sit around from then
until the next morning. And I have done that on occasion, right? I

do my weights. I do my workouts. I have my own routine that I do to keep me somewhat in shape. And it helps with my stress and stuff like that.

A lot of the time I dump the stress out on the guards or the case workers. A lot of the times I use self-talk. And I try and analyze what's going on. I use that most of all. Analyze it and ask is this important, or is this just about nothing. A lot of the time it just comes down to nothing. I come to grips with it and look at it. That's my mainstay in dealing with my stress. I tried getting drugs from the doctor; not what they call bug juice; not things like Chlorpromazine, or any of that, just some relaxants. They won't give you Valium here, so there's things underneath Valium that aren't as strong, but they won't give me any.

I do some drawing, art work, but not much, because I've lost motivation just being here. Play pool somewhat, but that's getting boring again. I've only been back here three months and sometimes I don't even feel like going down there. There's the school. That's kind of almost like a job, to get some sort of pay.

School on the street? Just wanting to get out. I wouldn't consider myself a bad student. I did most of my work anyway. But I was definitely disruptive in the classrooms. A cut-up at times. Sometimes I'd do things just to piss the teacher off. Or I wouldn't even show up sometimes. School to me was a harness.

So we'd go four-by-fouring, this was senior high, or just go out in the bush. We were a bunch of bush bunnies. I enjoyed fishing, canoeing, camping, hunting; anything like that – playing sports, football and that sort of stuff.

I played volleyball in school, for the school team, and was fair at that. Our team was fifth in BC, in the BC Winter Games. I played hockey, I played rugby, tennis, golf, played just about every sport.

I was always doing something, just whatever happened to be happening at the time. I had a buddy and he'd call up and say, let's go do this, or I'd call him and say, let's go do this – whatever come to mind at the time. We'd ride bikes; we had caves to explore. Most of the time we were trucking around in the bush. It wasn't much of a town. And we lived two miles out of town anyway.

My parents? Well, I didn't get along really well with my dad. He beat me. We were both kind of very similar in personality, as I see it now. And, like two negative ends of a magnet, we just don't mix. And he was only home weekends most of the time. Normally, we had one fight a week. Not physical, but an argument. My mom, she had a hard time in between us.

We did pretty good financially. Upper middle class I would say. We never really had a want for anything, except the extras. I had a ten-speed.

I got my first job when I was sixteen, right. And I had my driver's licence. It was an excuse to get my parents to get me my driver's licence. It was delivering pizzas. I did that for a while, but I got tired of it.

Intermittently, I'd go work for my dad out in the bush logging. He had his own logging show. We could work together. I don't know, that's one thing he gave me I guess, the ability to, when there was work to do, to do the work. I don't mind hard work, never have. So we worked together. He hired me about nine times. Nothing major.

In the mean time I was training to be a manager for Woolworth's. I did that for a while. I did some special things like clean out the stockroom once. I mean it was a big store. The stockroom was as big as the store. I spent two weekends taking it apart, cleaning it, painting it, putting it all back together in nice order and everything. I came in on a Monday morning, the assistant manager was taking credit for it. I was standing around the corner listening to it. And I came around the corner and said, well, I can't deal with this. Just the whole mentality of the brown-nosing effect. I couldn't fit in with that. Basically, logging was my job.

I played up to Junior B hockey and then I had that choice: I could play semi-professional hockey for nothing, or work for my dad logging and make $300 a day. So I took the money, right?

I probably would still be in logging, but, you know, I always wanted to invest, open other businesses, quick-money-turnaround kind of ideas, right, that I was never able to do. I think I would have done that. I was working towards that when I got arrested.

What happened, basically, was I was drinking in a bar. I'd just split up with my girlfriend a week earlier. I was out of work. My money was running out rapidly, but of course I had to keep partying. I was in the bar. Nine o'clock I ran out of money. I had a little money in the bank, but I couldn't get to it, so I decided to go – I don't even know if I decided that, right? I went out to look for more money. To see if I could borrow some, even. If I could have borrowed some, I probably wouldn't be here, right?

I ended up cruising the back of the motel where there was glass sliding doors, looking for purses or wallets sitting on the desks or dressers. I saw the purse. The door was open and I went in to get it. I didn't see anybody in the room. It was pretty easy. I think that was the first time I ever broke into a house. In fact, that's the only time I've broken into a house. I had the purse and I was heading out the door. A woman came out of the washroom, it was only a room and a washroom. I walked twenty feet into that room, grabbed the purse and headed out. And I didn't know anybody was in the washroom. I don't believe I was being quiet, you know? But the woman grabbed onto the purse. She was naked. She came with the purse and I was in, I guess, an aroused state. The adrenaline, just from going in there I guess, was up, and then this woman grabbing the purse, everything just kind of started pumping and going about three times the speed of light. She got knocked out, because she flew with the purse, because I just yanked trying to take it. And she just came with the purse and she hit her head on the dresser, knocked her out, and I kind of sitting there like shocked, and I get aroused and away we go, right?

From there it's just like … it's pretty hard to explain. Again it's RPC stuff – you know thinking errors and justifications and rationalizations, you know, a belief system that I had at the time. You know, I just really didn't care too much for anybody at that point, so it didn't matter what I did. I had no idea about jail. The thought never even occurred to me. After the rape, fear set in and I intended to knock the woman out and I hit her too hard and she died. And that kind of leads up to where I am here.

After I was sentenced? A lot of fear I would say, because of the rumours about prison. It was such a bad place. You know the old TV shows . . what prison is like. I came to Kent thinking that was what prison was like. You know, if you got in somebody else's way, you got stabbed, you got piped, you got whatever. This was my idea of what prison was like. When I came here, well, as I walked into the institution I had a guy threaten to kill me. And I had the butter-flies coming. It was just the fear of coming here, I guess you'd say.

You know, I would have preferred at that time to go to where he was and ask him what his problem was. I did have an attitude of sorts. But that's just me. That's not because of my sentence or any-thing. You know, if you want to threaten me, I'm not going to go hide and wait for you to get me when I'm not looking. But I couldn't get to him, because he couldn't function. He was a non-functioning type of inmate. He was in the hole because he feared other people who were out to get him. So, because of my charge I guess – it was front page for twenty-one days or something like that – he figured he'd build up his own self-esteem by threatening me. But anyway, I figured I was going to die in prison.

My parole date? I don't have a parole, a minimum parole date, except for twenty-five. There's a judicial review after I serve fifteen years, if I apply for it. They look at the crime. They look at what you've done in jail, and the changes that you've made, and if they decide to let you out on the street on passes, they want to know are you just going to go and screw up? And what they can do there is lower my minimum parole date, right? They can lower it right to fif-teen. That doesn't necessarily say that the parole board is going to let me out. It has nothing to do with the parole board until after. For me it feels pretty bleak at times. You know, I think, why am I being such a nice guy. Why do I let people get away with what they get away with? You know, they say well, you got this in fifteen years. And in fifteen years they tell me to beat it. You know, I took all the crap and all that for fifteen years. I really wonder what I'm going to think if they say that. What I'm going to be like, you know?

When I see guys getting out, my one thought is, they'll be back. I keep thinking that I wish I had that opportunity. I've never done time before this. You know, I've gone from not doing time to doing the most a person can do in a Canadian prison. I see the guys getting out and I think, good they're getting out, because this place is a nowhere. This is nowhere to live your life. I see them get out, but then I see at least 80 percent of them come back in. I've seen some guys five, six, seven times, out and in. Some coming back in on a parole violation, like suspected of drinking. To me it seems just really useless. It's just a big sardine can. Control of the uncontrollable.

If I were the judge? Personally, I'd send me to the nuthouse. Ah, geeze, I never really thought about that personally. It's really hard to say from this position because when I was out on the street without a record, guys like Clifford Olson, Campbell from back East, you know I'd hear about them and, you know, I'd think they should be tortured actually. In that sense, you know, beaten upon, abused tremendously. But now I'm in that position, somewhat, it's hard to say, because I don't want to be abused. In fact I fight a lot so I don't get abused – I don't physically fight.

Before I went to RPC I didn't care at all any more. Any time somebody did something or I perceived somebody doing something to me, I would rebel right there on the spot. So, if somebody bothers you, it doesn't matter what you do to him, because life is over, right. You could beat on him, whatever. The biggest saying in here is (of course it's not the lifers who are saying it): when you're doing life-25, you have nothing to lose. You can't lose any more. They can't do anything else to you.

I kind of like the sentencing of the States where they go, okay, it's a first-degree murder charge, give him ten to life. Ten years is a long time in prison, but you know, I'm two years short of it, and it's gone pretty quick. A life-25 sentence doesn't seem to have an end to it. You have no definite time to get out. So it's like giving a guy a licence to kill. You know, for the first one you did, you got life imprisonment. Then you could kill anybody and it wouldn't matter a smitten. Once you cross that line it doesn't matter where you are.

I think that the public, or whoever sets the sentence, knows that when you give a person life imprisonment, he tends to have the idea, like, my life's over. But you either kill yourself, which happens quite a bit, or you go the complete opposite and fight for everything, or kill somebody else. So the government put in a judicial review after fifteen years, a carrot. I mean there's three guys gone up on it, two have had their possibility for parole date reduced, and one has been told to go up a creek.

One killed a cop and he got reduced to fifteen, and one killed a child, ten or eleven-year-old child, and the third one, the one that got told to hit it, killed a cop as well.

I've never been able to focus on fifteen, so I just focus on twenty-five. I didn't see much at all. It really doesn't look that much different now. Actually it does, you know. I like to think it does. I guess there's a little bit of hope there, because I've done some of the RPC programs. You know, I've worked on my problems. And I actually feel pressed, because I want to get this mathematics degree. And I'm actually pressed for time to do it before my fifteen-year review. I want to get that degree and I want to finish the RPC program. Like I've got almost eight years in and I figure the RPC program is two years and to get a master's in mathematics takes six years, right, so that's another eight years. That's past my date.

I'm really frustrated being in Kent because of it, because I feel the longer I stay in Kent, the less the likelihood of my getting that fifteen-year review, positively. Like getting something positive out of it. It's going to be, why was he kept in Kent for so long? Why was he in a maximum for so long? And I wonder why myself.

Here every day is the same, just about. The only difference for me is that during the week I come to school in the morning. And that's the only real difference. The weekend I sleep during the morning, most of the time. Unless I have a visit or something like that on Sunday. That's about once every couple of months, maybe. Quarterly, I would say. Then there's letters and stuff like that. During the day I'll get up about twenty after seven and just kind of lay around until it's time to come here to school, have a coffee, some light conversation about absolutely nothing important. I'm usually pretty grouchy in the morning. I wake up and look at where I'm at every morning and that tends to weigh down on you after a while. I get quite annoyed at people that get up happy in the morning. I don't want to hear about it.

Anyway, I'll come here to school. A lot of the time I feel bored here at school, except when there's a . . like this morning we had that conversation. In all reality it means nothing to me, but it's interesting, right? Let the thoughts work in some kind of pattern that are just random. Then we go back about eleven and we have lunch. We'll be locked up first for a count, then lunch time. After lunch I usually play – just about every day – a game of bridge. That's an experience few will forget. There's a lot of arguing and venting, pretentiousness, and all that sort of stuff. I find that fairly hard to deal with coming from RPC and knowing why a person's doing that now, right? Sometimes I just get frustrated and I'll pick up and quit and say, find somebody else. I don't want to deal with this today. But usually we'll play the bridge and that being over, I'll do some school work I have to do; I'll do some reading; I'll do some of my art work; I'll just sit back and watch TV. It depends. I do a little carving, but I don't have any tools right now. If I had the tools I'd probably be doing that more than anything. But I haven't been able to make the money to order them. At RPC they had the tools, so I didn't have a need to buy them. So, that's basically the afternoon.

Then around four o'clock or quarter after four, somewhere around in there, we'll get locked up again for count; then supper. And then we go to the gym and do our workout. It's only rarely I miss my workout. Sometimes I stay back because my roommate will be going to the gym and that will give us time apart. I'll have, say, an hour and a half to be alone. They'll just lock the door. Most of the time I'll just lie on my bed and stare at the ceiling. Get some peace and quiet for a change. But normally I go and work out, go to the library. Our library and gym time are the same. Come back from the gym about six.

I'll get asked about four times to go play bridge. Sometimes I'll play, sometimes I won't. Most of the time is just spent doing nothing – most of the time. You're lucky if you get into a good conversation and that'll last two or three hours. We'll just sit back – three or four guys – and pick on each other and laugh at our little inconsistencies, stuff like that. And watch a movie or something on TV – videos, we have videos most every day. And at eleven o'clock it's *Sports Page*, *Arsenio Hall*, and after that I'm gone for the night, basically. That's a real normal day. That's like day in day out.

Oh, you've got all types of guys at Kent, guys from the SHU [Special Handling Unit] in PC that have either flipped out or done something in the prison like, took a guard hostage, or piped somebody, or stabbed somebody, or whatever. We have those people here in protective custody – very unstable types.

Actually they're more my friends than any of the other guys. They're more honest; they're more unstable, but they're more honest. They don't play head games with me; they don't try and manipulate me, or threaten me, or whatever. We seem to get along; we can relate.

And then there's pedophiles. They're meek, mild, fearful. I can get along with them, but they don't understand me as a person. And I can understand them being at RPC and being in the program with a number of pedophiles. I understand that they have problems, just like I have problems, right? It doesn't sit right with me, their crime, but I look at mine and that doesn't sit right with me either, right? It's hard not to be judgmental about them or about myself – either way. I guess I try not to associate with that group.

And then there's the rapists. I guess I would fit into that category in a sense, because there was sex involved in the crime. My crime was more a crime of violence, I would say. And control, power. Remember the old saying, power corrupts and absolute power corrupts absolutely. And sure enough, right?

There are guys that are in protective custody for poker debts in the general population. You know, they played poker with no money and then the guys want to collect, and then they come into PC because they're fearful for their lives.

Then there's the rats. They would fit, as far as the totem pole goes, on the very bottom. They would be the packing to hold the totem pole in. That kind of idea. They're the people I don't get along with at all. I don't even tolerate them being around me. If they are around me, if I can leave, I will. I would prefer they left. I don't lend things to them. I don't tell them anything. I don't have any dealings with them if I can at all help it, because I really don't approve at all of how they live their life. They benefit from hurting others. And that's why I'm in jail, because I hurt somebody else. I see them as the reason I'm still here in Kent.

I've just put a transfer in for Mission Institution. Hopefully I'll get transferred to Mission. In all reality I should have been there two years ago, three years ago, in the normal routine of things. For some reason I've been waylaid, and the only consistent thing that I see is that when things happen in the unit, when they come to me and ask me what happened, they don't get any information. Some of the other boys that have been transferred were willing to give this information.

To me, it's more what I've grown up with, right? All my life. They say it's a con code, but I don't come from a criminal background. None of my friends have ever been in jail, so it's just kind of an attitude I think. If you want to do it, you can do it, but not me. If a friend of mine or something got into trouble, I'd be there to back him up, to help him out if possible. You know, be it calmly or violently to a certain degree. So, they look at that, I think, and they call it a con code. So I'm stuck in Kent.

I can't go to Mountain, because of a man who has done some things to me before I came to Kent, when I was in provincial. He tried to set me up for some things, etcetera, etcetera. And at one point I verbally threatened him with physical harm, right. That was quite a ways back, but he's still scared of it. He has told the authorities in Mountain that he thinks I'm going to come over and kill him, or whatever he said, I don't know. They're not going to take a chance. Plus he's one of those guys who will give information. They use him to benefit security. They get too much out of him. He's useful, right? And I'm useless, right?

The only thing that I can see as far as the programs, before I can ever get a parole, is the sex offender program at RPC, which I've done over half of. But that will be a prerequisite for me. They say it's an eighteen-month program, but there's no way on this earth that you could finish it in eighteen months.

The reason I went there and I left is I could have finished the program quite easily, but it wouldn't have done me any good at that point. So I left until I get a little more motivation to go past a certain point, right. To get past some barriers that I have.

I regret what I did. I always will. Not completely for the victim, but for myself as well. I regret what I did and being where I am. I at times wake up with nightmares, reliving the crime. It's still there. But I think that's because I just came back from RPC, partially. You know, there's nothing I can do to change it. I definitely feel sorry about it, right? I should point out that at RPC one of my biggest problems is not being able to forgive myself. So, when I forgive myself for doing what I did, which I've done, does that mean I have no remorse? If you can forgive yourself, how can you have remorse? I don't understand that. They have to be able to look at that and say, okay, he's done what he's done, this is what he's doing to make sure it doesn't happen again. But you can't make positive gains if you keep getting down on yourself, right? It just doesn't work that way. If you keep telling yourself, I'm no good, why even attempt school or anything? Because you're always going to be no good in your own mind.

I'm doing this thing for school, a journal. I'm doing a journal for seven days. I've noticed in those seven days, the same thing comes up. It's morally wrong to try and control people, but when fears come into that, like when, say, society fears, with a good right, feared me and what I did, I understand that. But the first thing they try and do is take all control. My crime is because I had no control in my life, I felt no control over my life. Everybody else seemed to be controlling what I was doing. So I committed my crime. That's a simple way of saying it. So they say because I can't control myself, that I should be controlled. And that's the main reason I did my crime in the first place – to get some sort of control over my life. I mean it was definitely the wrong way to go about things, but I was trying to control. I was trying to have some sort of control over something in my life – and somebody else. I felt everybody else controlled me, so I should be able to do this.

At this point in time, I don't see myself as any different from anybody, except I kind of stopped maturing. I mean, I was only twenty years old when I committed my crime. I stopped maturing emotionally, I would say mostly. I guess my interaction with women kind of stopped with the sexual part. I was using a lot of drugs. It's easier for me to name the drugs I haven't used. I mean heroin, opium, angel dust. And that, I can see for sure, halted a lot of my emotional growth, because I didn't want to deal with any of my problems, or my feelings about, you know, family troubles with my dad, say. I couldn't talk to him and he couldn't talk to me either. We were both just talking to a wall. So, if we had a big fight, or whatever, I'd just go smoke a joint and everything was better; just ignore the problem.

So, just by ignoring all these problems, I didn't go through them and learn how to deal with them. So it got to a point where I hadn't been dealing with my problems and my little annoyances and angers, and they just built up, finally you can't hold them in anymore.

I see them as seeing me as fairly calm, respectful of a person as a person, wanting to progress on my problem; wanting to get out of jail. But they see me as lacking in vocational skills. It's the first specific thing I have problems with. To me vocational skills is the ability to work – to do different jobs. I have vocational skills, I feel, more than the people writing these reports. I can run any piece of heavy machinery you want to put in front of me. I'm a logger, I've driven logging trucks, cats, loaders, chain saws, skidders. You know, I can take them apart and put them back together and they'll still run. I don't have any degrees, but I have the skills. But they see me as lacking vocational skills.

Well, on the street, I better be working for myself. I always wanted to in the first place, and I can't see having some boss holding my life in his hands. You know, if he fires me and I don't have any work … it's hard enough to get a job without a record, but with a record of being a murderer, sex offender on top of it, it would be near impossible to get a job. And the guy that's going to hire you is going have a lot of, you know, you either do this or you don't work at all. I'm second-guessing this. You know, myself, I have a goal of getting a doctorate in mathematics, right, but I also like to learn languages. I'd like to be a cabinetmaker. I think that's a job that'll be around forever.

I don't know as I want to do any physical labour, because I'll be around forty-six years old. I don't think I'll be wanting to run chain saws anymore, or packing bricks or moving cement around. I enjoy working. I like artwork, carving. If I could make that into a trade for myself, I would. That would be a major goal. I'd give my eye teeth to get out just so I can work. If I had a job to go to I would go every day just to get out of here. It's a dead-end street, right?

Personally I don't think prisons are worth the money they put out to keep them. I'm sure there has to be prisons, but they know that ninety percent of sex offenders have been sexually abused. Eighty percent of all crimes have alcohol and drug involvement in them. They pay sixty-five, seventy thousand dollars a year just to keep us here; each guy. That's what it works out to. That's an incredible amount of money. Why don't they give the guys that're looking for money, give them half and they wouldn't be in here.

One other major thing I'd change is double-bunking. Institutions are going to be here; but double-bunking is something I would change. That takes a person down; dehumanizes people. I was thinking about it yesterday, as a matter of fact. My roommate was eating his meal on the desk and I had to go to the washroom at the same time, just urinate, but, you know, it just strikes me as that's not right. It's dirty. Those are the things you have to go through day after day here.

UPDATE

Terry was transferred to Mission in 1990 and it was "definitely more enjoyable." In 1991 he returned to RPC to finish his program and was now returned to his "home" institution of Mission where this interview took place in 1995. His judicial review was coming up in two years and he was simultaneously "looking forward to it" and also "very tentative" and "scared." He felt that a number of positive changes had occurred, that he was "growing up" and now "did not take out his anger on others" (in this regard he thought the RPC sex offenders program had been of real help). He had been married in 1992, but the relationship was "on the rocks now." His wife came from "a very dysfunctional background" and he wasn't able to give her the support she needed, so she sought it elsewhere. He had levelled with her from day one and she had been fully aware of why he was serving time. He lost interest in the university courses he'd been taking by correspondence. He saw his family three to five times a year and was getting along better with his father. He believed that the "big-time difference" between Mission and Kent was that the staff saw prisoners as people and could talk to them. "I can control me, let's put it that way." He wanted to write about the whole life-25 sentencing formula. In his view, the last ten years of such a sentence were just "drugs for the public," to keep them believing that something was being done, that they were "safe." He thought the sentence should focus more on therapy than retribution. Coming from his family background with its dysfunctional relationships, he "just didn't know." Now he was "just living my life": he wanted to "just get out and mow the lawns, do the things I used to hate doing."

'If I haven't earned my freedom, then don't set me free.'

William was thirty-one when sentenced to life-25. He had served thirteen years at the time of the interview.

My sentence right now? I see a lot of hope. Why do I see hope? Well, I'm at the lowest possible security that the system has to offer. I am one step from the community today. And I feel that I am here because I've earned my way here. I want to go back into the community, not because you gave it to me, but because I earned it. You see, I believe that, and I've lived that. If I haven't earned this, then what am I doing here? If I haven't earned my freedom, then don't set me free.

Well, I just started being more realistic, more helpful; and when I say helpful, when prisoners came in and had problems inside the system, I started helping these individuals. And what happened is that, even though I helped these people, I did it for myself. I learned that later on. I didn't really do it for them at all. I did it for me.

I helped, literally, fifty, sixty people out, while I was in Kent, and then I went on to Matsqui and I did it tenfold. You know, it ended up hundreds of people I helped out. But the thing is, what I got back was a different kind of respect, and good feelings. They were positive strokes. People said, oh, you're a good guy, and deep inside I felt good about that. I felt really wonderful that somebody could see some good in me. And inside, I said, well, I can't be all that bad. You know, if these people could see some good, I must be a good person, and I just responded to that. I responded beyond words.

I went and founded a group in Matsqui for the handicapped – retarded people. They were people that I brought in from the community. They didn't ask what I was in for; they were only interested in one thing and that was whether I would get them a cup of water, or coffee, and whether he was good enough that way. And those people, over a three-year period, showed me they loved me. They showed me so many times that they loved me, and what happens is, love begets love.

You know, I never knew I had feelings. I didn't think I had feelings, but these people brought that out in me, and when I say to you that today I feel very, very strong that I deserve the sentence I got, I believe that. I believe that I have to be segregated from society, for whatever length of time they feel that I need to be, until I'm fit to come back into it. I do not believe the twenty-five-year minimum is the answer to it. I believe that it doesn't matter whether you have a five-year minimum, or a twenty-five-year minimum, if you're a real horrible person, you're not going to get out no matter what you have.

A life sentence is a life sentence. I think the twenty-five-year minimum is nothing more than it creates more desperate people – hopelessness. For about five or six years, maybe seven years, I went through a time where there was no hope. I felt that there was nothing to live for. I was a walking and talking dead man as far as that was concerned, because there was nothing, no hope – despair, you know, and negativity all around you – and the thought of violence continuously crossing your mind. When you're living in that kind of environment, you become like an animal. And, that's why some men, they never change, they never escape from that.

You know, until I was about thirty-eight, the system thought I was probably one of the most dangerous men in Canada. And, there's probably many, many staff in Kent Institution that feel I'm still the worst animal walking this earth. My files contain nothing but violence, anger, hate, rebellion, anti-social behaviour, you name it. It shows there's a very dangerous man there. The only thing I have to counteract act that is that there's been a real positive influx. Now, because now we have two files, we have one that's about two feet thick of negativity, and we have a small one that's growing every year that's about six inches of positivity. I want people to look at the positive things, because I freely admit the negative part. You see, I don't deny that, I don't deny one thing that's in them files. That did happen. But, look today at who I am now, not who I was. I say to you, and I say to anybody, I was a very dangerous man at one time. And why was I dangerous? Because I believed lies, and I accepted garbage and bullshit and I literally thought I was living it! You know, I lied so much that I believed it, and that's the truth, and that's why I'm in prison.

The first time I was incarcerated I was fourteen years of age. I was put in a boys school, Bowenville Training School, because at that time there was no more foster homes, so they incarcerated me in a juvenile delinquents school. I was there about fourteen months. I was released into a halfway house in Toronto, and that was a group home. But unfortunately this was a horrible, horrible house. It was nothing more than a playground for a homosexual, so I ran away from there, and I got incarcerated again within a matter of days for B&Es, theft, and things like that, and I was taken back to Bowenville. I was there about eleven months the second time. That put me back on the street about when I was sixteen years of age. In August of the next year, I got arrested for assault causing bodily harm and robbery, and I ended up in the Guelph Reformatory – my first bit in a provincial system for adults.

I was there for ten months the first time. I was released and within a matter of days I was re-arrested for assault causing bodily harm. I got two years less a day. And, again it was provincial. From there I was transferred to a place called OTS Guelph, which is the super-maximum for troubled delinquents. You know, with hardcore delinquents. And from OTS Guelph, I was transferred to Millbrook Reformatory, which is supposedly the hard-core for reformatory inmates. I did about eight months there. I was able to con my way out of there. Told them I was an alcoholic and I was sent to a place called Mimico which was the drunk tank at the time, and I was released within a couple of weeks. I was arrested again and I got two years for assault causing bodily harm.

I guess I was twenty by the time I reached the penitentiary. I did two years on the first one, and I was released and within twenty one days I got arrested for assault. Two charges of attempted murder this time, and I got two more years for that offence.

The only thing I knew was prisons. The only people I knew were people I met while I was incarcerated. I knew absolutely nobody else on earth, nothing was ever offered to me in the form of support in the community. And what little was offered, because of the role we were playing, I couldn't accept at that time. And that's the truth. By the time I was seventeen, eighteen years of age, it was us against them, and I didn't want to go to them and say, hey, lookit, I've got nothing out there, I don't have any home, I don't have any family. No way.

I would usually use drugs, alcohol abuse and drugs, and hang around with street people and stuff like that. These same people, by the way, were the people that I met in jail. This was the truth. That's the truth right there. Many of the people I associated with in the community were people I met either in Bowenville, or Guelph, and, as I grew older, Kingston Penitentiary – you know, the big boys! The thing is, that when I came into these places, I am going to say this and I want that stressed, I came in a young boy. I had no one that cared for me; I had no home; no one wanted me, and that's the reason why I was brought into the system, because the Children's Aid Society thought they were doing me a favour. They brought me in and exposed me to criminals, people that had broken the law. And because of peer pressure, I accepted those values, and I became a criminal out of the need of being accepted by somebody. And I was accepted by these criminals, petty criminals like myself. They were no better than myself, but, to ourselves, we were something.

The first time I went to Kingston Penitentiary I was twenty years of age. The reason why I know that is because I went to the penitentiary because I was drinking in a bar in Toronto, and a guy asked me for my ID, and in those days you had to be twenty-one years of age. And because I had no ID, a fight erupted. I assaulted this man with an axe, and I ended up going back to the penitentiary for that.

And the thing is – here's what it is – a lot of men come into these places and you might be just an ordinary Joe when you come in, but out of wanting to be accepted by your peers inside these places, you tend to build yourself up, to be more than you really are. And eventually, eventually, you begin to believe that crap. You start saying, oh yeah, oh I'm a real bad guy. By the time I reached Archembeault, in the seventies, I had convinced myself that I was a successful armed robber, and there was no buts and no maybes. Sure, I done a few, but they were petty, nothing, maybe for a hundred bucks. But by the time I got to the pen, it was up to two or three thousand. We always exaggerated our scores.

Most of my offences were committed when I was intoxicated. Ninety-nine percent of the things I committed I couldn't remember, because I was under the influence of some drug or some booze. And the attacks I committed, they said they were very ferocious, very vicious and angered. And I'm going to say that all that is true – that was true – but that was that little boy striking out at the world, trying to get even. I believe that with all my heart.

I've wrote a book on this. I call myself Nobody's Child in that book, and the reason I picked Nobody's Child, because I was nearly thirty-nine years old, was that that was one feeling that I always had, that I was nobody's. I came into this world, nobody claimed me, nobody wanted me.

My family? I had no family. I've had no family right from when I came into this world. My mother tried to kill me when I was two weeks old, and I was put in the Children's Aid Society. Was in fourteen different foster homes. By the time I was aged thirteen, the longest I stayed at one house or one group home was from eleven till I was about thirteen and a half, fourteen years of age. That's the longest. I went to jail when I was fourteen.

So anyway, so, I was in Kingston. I was twenty years of age. I ended up in a fight with another individual; I hit him with a crowbar, and I was transferred to the super-max in Quebec which, in them years, it was supposed to house the hardest men in Canada. This was the first SHU, but we called it the super-max in them days. I was one of the first people in there, and me and some of my childhood buddies, we all showed up there. And that's when we said, well, hey, we made it. We're in the big time now, you know, because we looked around and we saw some of the hardest names in Canada standing there, and we said, well, here we are, we're here with them.

From there I was transferred, no, I got released out of the super-max. This was in February, and nine weeks later, the first week of May, I got arrested for some armed robberies in Toronto, and I was given an eight-year sentence in the penitentiary for a $150 armed robbery.

It was awful, awful expensive. We add that up, you know? That's unbelievable that a man would want to spend eight years of his life, waste his life, for $150. But it happened, and I went back to Kingston Penitentiary.

Now, as I mentioned, I was shipped out of Kingston to the super-max, the last time I was in, for hitting a guy over the head with a crowbar. Well, when I arrived back, that individual's in the institution, and there was all kinds of threats, that they were going to kill me and all this sort of stuff. But, we were able to overcome that, me and a buddy of mine. We confronted this individual. Nobody got hurt, and the nice part about it was that, from then on, I was a somebody in the penitentiary system because I confronted this person, who had forty men against myself, and I was able to walk away— and no man was ever able to do that. And, the thing is, from that day forth, I was no longer the nobody, I was a somebody who could beat anybody, who could stare down and, if necessary, fight the whole group. And, for many many months, I tried to live that.

Five months after this confrontation, I got into a fight with two guards. I punched one out and I only slapped the other one because he was an older man, and I got two years, three months added onto my eight-year sentence. I was transferred from there to Collins Bay, because during my incarceration in the hole, two individuals kidnapped two shop instructors and demanded my release. That was one of the first kidnappings in Canada and because I was involved, I was transferred from Collins Bay to the super-max in Quebec, which is just outside Laval. I did nineteen months there, and then I was transferred to Archembeault, which is the meanest and best prison I've ever been in in my life in Canada.

Why do I say the best? Well, I'll tell you. You met all the elite criminals in the world. As far as I was concerned, there was no greater criminals than the Frenchmen. They were the greatest bank robbers and all that and it was just wonderful to go there. You know, I thought well, this was the elite. I'm going to Archembeault with all the tough guys. And, oh man, you know, I went there living the illusion and met many of the people that were famous in Quebec. I met them all, all the good guys, and some of the Devil's Disciples [a motorcycle gang].

The thing was, I was a nobody in Archembeault, but I felt so good being in their presence that I was able to, you know, in my own mind, justify this and say, well, I'm one of these guys now, you know? I'm one of these; I've finally made it; I'm now the top. And I start telling all my friends, I'm going to rob Brinks trucks now; I've got no choice. I've got to go out and rob some Brinks trucks, you know? That's what all us elite people do. So, for about five or six years I sat in there and I kept convincing myself that robbing and killing was right, because that was what I was surrounded by.

After seven years – I was thirty-one – I was released. I never made a parole out of all these bits, because I had nothing to offer, and because I had nothing, I was too ashamed to go up to them and say, well, I don't have a family, I don't have anyone that wants to help me. And because I was so caught up in this trip, this me against them, I refused to come forward. But I'd met a man while I was incarcerated, a man who professed to be a Christian. He visited me for three years solid, and he promised me the moon. He promised me I could live in one of his houses. He'd fix up the basement and I could live there upon my release. And he said, take six months. Take your time to get used to living like a citizen again. But upon my release, he started lying to me the moment I got in the car. By the time we reached downtown Montreal, he told me outright that I couldn't come to his house. And when he said that, all hopes of ever going straight were gone.

Within two hours, I was armed with a shotgun. And within four days I was pulling scores again, and within a matter of three weeks I had shot a person accidentally. It was in a bank robbery, and in the commandeering of a car. I say accidentally because there are circumstances in my mind that say it was accidental. I did not go out that day with the intent to murder this person. I did not do that. I went out with the intent to rob a bank, and I freely admit that in my mind, I was willing to shoot, but I did not want to kill anybody. And, unfortunately, a young person lost her life, because of my stupidity. And I got a twenty-five-year minimum, this time. I pleaded guilty to second-degree murder, but I still got a twenty-five year minimum.

But you know, at the moment that he gave me the sentence, I didn't care. I didn't care one hoot, because I didn't know anybody outside. I felt more comfortable inside than I did outside. I knew people in jail, people that cared for me, and I didn't have anywhere else to go. When that man said twenty-five years, it didn't dawn on me that it was twenty-five years. I just thought, oh well, I'm out of circulation for a while, you know? Because you see, when you get caught up in the system, it doesn't dawn on you. Time means nothing to you.

Three years later, I started changing. And I think what brings about change is the realization of how violent this world is, how unpredictable it is. Some of the riots we've had, some of the disturbances I've been in. I mean, we have literally torn buildings apart for the fun of it. No rhyme or reason. You know, I can see us doing something for a reason, but when you literally destroy buildings, and sometimes people, for no reason, you know, it starts to dawn on you, that hey, what kind of world are we living in? I was in Kent Institution at the time, and I would say that I was very well respected. I was the chairman of the Inmate Committee. I'd been involved in almost every group in Kent at the time. And I'd negotiated an awful lot for the prisoners. Yes, oh yes, I was still a high risk. That was the reason I was elected as the chairman of the committee. But when I saw my friends, many people I've known in the past getting stabbed, and heard about people in the East being murdered, friends of mine, people I'd really respected, all the old-timers, violent guys that had lived by the gun, I said, wow, man, they're all getting killed, you know?

Then, in Kent, reality really came when a friend of mine wanted to chase a young kid into PC for no reason. Didn't even know this kid. And I sensed right there and then, at that very moment, I could be a victim. One day I would be a victim. And I decided right there and then, that if I was going to be a victim, that I was going to do something about it today.

You know, there's an old saying here. There's only three ways out of this system: you can retire and walk the other way; or you can walk out of here and live on welfare, be a wino and a beggar, or you can end up dead. And I've seen thousands of men go out and be the winos and the leeches in the bars and live on welfare, and all that crap. I've seen many of my dear friends, people that I've really respected through the years, people all the other cons in Canada respect, that ended up dead because they didn't want to change. But I said, well, I want to beat them.

You know at one time I read a book, it was by Che Guevara. And Che Guevara said that if you let the system stand still, no matter who you are, you'll become exactly like the people you want to oust. And I believe that. I believe that because today I accept the same values as the system has. I accept that there's wrong and there's right; I accept that there's some good people and there's bad people. I also believe that the bad people have to be segregated from society. I believe that very strongly today where I didn't at one time.

You know, after wasting nearly thirty years of my life in prison, I've been in the community roughly eleven months. And the thing is, I believe that if people are in the same frame of mind I was in, at the time of the shooting, they should not be released from prison under any circumstances. I had only one thought in mind, and that was to rob banks, and, if necessary, kill people for that money. I was in a horrible, horrible state of mind, but I was able to get by because, you see, they had to let me out. That's the problem. They have to let people out. And today, after thirty years in the system, I say that's totally wrong. It's horrible, horrible.

I believe that the system is going to have to change to the point where people are going to have to be given indefinite sentences for certain offences. And the reason why I say that is, I would love to see the day come where a new system is implemented, you could call it the merit system.

If you come in here and nothing's here for you, well you become gloomy, you become depressed; you become dangerous. But, if you walk into this system and they say, listen brother, you show us this and this and this, we're going to give you consideration to let you out again. We, the people, will give you another opportunity, but you have to earn it. And if you don't want to earn it, then you're going to sit here until you bloody well do. You see if everything's given to people, they can hide in these systems and still be the dangerous man that comes back into the community and harms a person like I did. You know, when you say harm, you can't harm a person more than killing someone like I did for no reason. There's nothing more horrible than that, and the thing is that the system, I don't care what people say, the system is to blame because they let me out. They didn't know me from Adam. I'm saying that the system has to change to the degree that they know the individuals, and if they don't know the guy, then the guy stays until they do.

For myself, I felt that if I was going to get out of the system alive, I was going to have to change. I took a look at my life and it wasn't a very pretty picture. I went to my house one day and I sat down and I said, well, how many friends do I really have? I added them all up and I didn't have anybody in the community. And I said, Well, who loves you? And again, I had nobody. I wasn't getting any letters. I wasn't getting any visits. I said, well what would happen if you died in here tonight? What would happen? The realization came that nobody would care. Nobody would even claim my body. It would go to the morgue and be buried in a pauper's grave with six other bodies. I became a number, and I would die a number.

That is a frightening, frightening thought, that you just become a number and nothing else in this world. I said that I didn't want that. So, I analyzed everything very, very careful. I started telling people that I was a failure as a criminal. I started saying that my whole life was a lie, that I had lied all them years, that I'd exaggerated, that I was literally a bum. I wasn't a good criminal at all, that just out of fear, for acceptance, I exaggerated my crimes. And the worst part about this is, they had believed me, and I had believed their garbage. You know what I'm saying?

Yeah, I started to tell everybody that. I felt that I owed that much. And I said that if I was really going to change, I was going to have to face reality and start telling them the truth.

And that's about everything in my life. You're either straight or you're not. You're either going to walk out of these places and never come back, or you're lying and you're going to come back. You know, for thirty years I lied about that. I told them I was a great criminal; I would never come back, but the reality was that I always came back. And now, at forty-three, I'm going to be forty-four in another two weeks, I want to show the world that if a man really gets the truth in himself, that he can turn around and walk away from here. And, and that is very, very important to me.

I'm in my thirteenth year. I'll be starting my fourteenth year in another month. And I would say, even if I'm very fortunate to win my review, I would say I'll do about twenty straight years of my life in prison. I'll be about fifty years of age before I'm free.

Oh, I've already got that worked out. I'm presently learning to be a very good chef. I love cooking. I also feel that I have something to offer in counselling. I could see myself in the capacity of a counsellor in a halfway house. I have a dear friend trying to get a halfway house, and if that happens he would love me to work there. I could see myself offering my services to almost any halfway house, or preferably an institution that deals with young offenders. I've been there, and I feel I have something I can offer. I cannot see myself holding down a tradesman job, because I've wasted my whole life. I can't see that. I can see myself lecturing in high schools and universities; I can see myself talking to group homes. And I honestly believe that I will be financed eventually by the system itself, and the reason why is because not many men have been able to do thirty-some years of their life in prison, and have still been youthful enough to be an asset to the system. I'll be fifty years of age, and I will have done an unbelievable length of time in prison, but I'll still have at least ten, fifteen years of service to render to somebody.

I don't feel for one second it's going to be very easy. And the reason why is it's hard for a man to start over as a child, to learn how to live again. You know, I don't know the first thing about fatherhood, I don't know a thing about parenting, I don't know how to treat a wife, I don't know how to work for myself, I don't how to support myself, I don't know how to budget money, you know? I'm trying to get something but at fifty years of age, and because of my background, I'm going to be limited to movement, and I don't blame them. You see what I'm saying.

Right now I think what the system has to do, and I mean this, you have to prepare the individual for the community. And that individual's got to prepare himself also. It's got to be a two-way program. For instance, education-wise, we have to live up to a standard in this country, so there's no reason why a man shouldn't use the system to benefit himself. He can learn trades while he's in. But as we get closer to the street, then that's where we have these pass programs. And I think passes should be structured for the sole purpose of this man trying to establish a support system for himself in the community, prior to his release. I don't think any man should ever be released unless he's got support out there. Unless he's got committed citizens that say, lookit, we're going to take this man under our wing and we're going to help him, then that man is at a risk of reoffending.

If you don't have that – yes, we have a few individuals that are coming from a classy kind of background – but the majority, eighty percent of us, are still from skids. We're from skid row, we're from the slums. We're from the broken homes. We didn't grow up with silver spoons in our mouths. And the thing is, that's where the criminals are coming from. When I say "criminals" – no, that's the wrong term. We're not criminals, we're bums, and we weren't arrested, we were rescued. You know, many of us didn't have anything out there, so we came in here. We get free meals, we get everything here, you know? That's the truth. So, if you want to have a real constructive program, then you're going to have to take these individuals and make them aware that we're for them to stay out of here, but they have to get something for themselves in the community.

You know, you can't take my hand and lead me around all my life. I got to do that myself, I've got to walk around. So, it's up to me to show the initiative and meet people, and accept their values. You see, if you won't accept their values, you're not going to fit in. That's the key, the values. Because you'll find out that many of the people that are returning, they have warped values. That's the only thing I can see.

To get community involvement in these places is the key. We're going to be returning back out there one day, and who should be more involved than the communities that we come from? They are the ones that should be aware that we're coming back out, and that there should be little groups in all these little towns and cities to say, lookit, we have a problem here. This man's coming back. What are we going to do about that? We can either accept him, or reject him. If we reject him, he's going to ... God only knows what he's going to do.

If you walk out of here and no one loves you, and no one cares about you, well you're going to go and find someone that does. And who's that going to be? Why, it's going to be one of your old buddies. It's going to be one of your old girls that are walking the streets. Because you don't know anybody else. So, that's the key. I feel that very strongly.

My church group comes into this institution every two weeks, on Friday nights, and during the other two weeks, people come individually to visit me. I've many, many families come and visit me. And there's AA. Those are the only things I'm really involved in. Oh, I'm also upgrading myself, yes. I'm two subjects away from accomplishing my Grade 12, which I feel is a real accomplishment on my behalf. And the nice part about that is, I'm doing this – the system didn't do it for me. I had to come forward and take the initiative. And I feel that's the way it should be.

You know, when you force people to do things, they don't enjoy it. But when someone comes forward on their own, it's because they want to do it, and they usually succeed. You see, that's what's nice about it, and that's why I feel that I'm going to pass in August. To most people it's nothing, but to me it's a real accomplishment, because that certificate will state that I have an equivalency of a Grade 12 person, and that's something I can feel proud of after all these years. If someone said, well, what did you do with yourself? Well, I got my Grade 12. T'isn't much, but it's something.

UPDATE

After a wait of two years, and a transfer to a Montreal-area minimum-security prison, William received the outcome of his fifteen-year review. "I won. It was dropped to life-22. I'll be eligible for parole next year, for day parole. I'm just starting my nineteenth year." William had predicted he would have to serve twenty years before being granted day parole.

Once the decision was rendered, he was returned to Elbow Lake Institution. His stay, however, was short lived. Within a few months of his arrival, he was sent to Kent Institution. "I was transferred out of camp basically because I loaned some tobacco out. I got shipped to Kent because somebody said I had an automatic weapon. It turns out that the individual owed me some money. The sad part is that although they know he lied, he won't get punished. But I'm still very, very much encouraged. It's not getting me down." William said he was also encouraged by the members of his church. "They're still very, very much involved in my life. They're coming here. They came to Montreal for me too."

According to institution sources, his transfer to Kent was not likely to affect his chances for day parole. Because of this William continued to plan for his imminent release. "I'm really interested in a slow, slow transition into the community. Someday I want to open up a ranch for long-term offenders. A ranch for the sole purpose of a slow transition into the community – maybe two years. But for now, I'm going to ask for day parole to Sumas Centre so I can go to Simon Fraser. I want to got to SFU as a mature student to get a drug and alcohol counselling certificate. I feel that's where my future is."

'When would enough be enough?'

Lance was nineteen when sentenced to life-25. He had served twenty years at the time of the interview.

When I first started doing time it was in Stoney Mountain in Manitoba, northeast of Winnipeg. And Stoney was limestone walls, maybe twenty-seven foot high. And everything, the entire building, is limestone. A lot of controlled areas. Four tiers high, big dome. Much the same fashion that BC Pen was. I also spent a little bit of time in BC Pen too. I'd say it's less restrictive here. It's a lot more laid back, less confining I would say.

I've been here in Mountain [Mountain Penitentiary in BC, not the same as Stoney Mountain] fifteen years out of twenty, in March. I've seen this place change a lot too. During the first few years there was just the one fence around and it lacked facilities, for example, lacked the library, lacked the school, lacked the gymnasium.

When I first came, I was in the kitchen for a short time. Everyone who comes to this institution goes to work in the kitchen. I spent about a year and a half in there. And then I think I went to work on the yard crew, the grounds crew. There wasn't a whole lot back then, but in that particular period of time I did a couple of correspondence courses – Grade 11 and Grade 12 bookkeeping. And it was that which got me probably one of my most productive jobs in here, working for NELOF Co-op.

NELOF stands for Native Extraordinary Line of Furniture. That was an inmate co-op that dealt with Northwest Coast art as well as furniture, and combining those two elements. They needed a bookkeeper at the time and, because of my bookkeeping courses, I was hired. That was in the winter of '76, the latter part of '76.

At first I didn't know anything about Northwest Coast art. But I began to carve, to learn how to work in wood as well as handle all purchases and sales, and everything to do with the office. I was one of the only guys that's ever had an office here, upstairs in the administration building, specifically for NELOF. We used to work through the finance department, and pay the bills once a month, and developed a line of credit, etcetera, etcetera. Initially, like I said, I was hired as a bookkeeper but shortly afterwards I was appointed to the board of directors. I was the secretary-treasurer of the board. Board of directors consisted of representatives from the inmate population, or the body of twenty-five guys that were working there, as well as outside sponsors. For example, Randy Merton, who has since deceased, who was in charge of AIM's [the American Indian Movement's] halfway house, he was on the board of directors. Sharon Martin was on, and the warden.

I quickly developed an interest in the art, which meant not only the actual working, but studying with the different tribes on the Northwest Coast. And that meant a lot of reading, and practising. It captured me so much that I was working virtually sixteen hours a day. There was from eight till four over at the shop, and then from four till midnight in my cubicle, or in the hut working with the guys. We'd take the projects home and we'd work at home, and it became a real close-knit group of people. A lot of us were living in

Hut 2 at that particular time and we just carried it on. In effect, I ended up doing a seven-year apprentice program in about three.

I started off with two-dimensional art: flat design, painting and carving two-dimensionally. I figured that if I learned everything there was to learn about two-dimensional art, somehow the rest of it would just naturally follow – the three-dimensional carving of totem poles, and masks, and all the rest of that. So I became a specialist in two-dimensional art. But for me, not only was it studying about the present-day opportunities – what was available in paints, and brushes, and all of the rest in the market – but I also learned how to make tools. I learned how to make knives, how to make adzes. I learned as well about what they used for the old paints, the kinds of pigments they had, and tried to find some kind of compatibility with the regular stuff that's on the market.

We used to do a lot of things at NELOF. It was more working together, a sharing of knowledge. We had people who had a lot of expertise, like Roy Peters and Andy Morris. Later on, we developed training courses and got outside experts to come in. Barry Rossiter would show us how to do curve-bent boxes, which became another one of my specialities later on. We had all kinds of thing that we'd do, lots of techniques developed. For example, there was learning how to adze properly. A lot of guys, they would just get there and bang away, rather than developing a rhythm according to their heartbeat, so they could work in unison with their heart and therefore allow them to work all day long. It takes a while to develop those kinds of things. It was a lot of fun at NELOF.

I worked there up until 1980. They finally shut us down because we were independent. We got cocky. We were totally independent, we did our own ordering and everything else. We had whatever we wanted and whatever we needed, and we paid for it, right? But there was virtually no control from the institutional aspect so they shut us down.

My Native background? Well, I'm from the prairies. My folks are

Métis – Cree and coureurs de bois. My great-grandfather helped erect the first church in Pine Falls. I grew up as a city kid in Winnipeg.

School on the street? The first thing that comes to mind was trying to go back after I had been getting into difficulty with the law. I had a real difficult time in high school. And it was after I had been out for about a year that I tried to go back and get into Grade 11. I couldn't go back. I couldn't go back and start where I left off. I tried to apply in several schools, but the schools weren't accepting me although inside I felt a desire to go back, I wanted to go back for probably the first time in my life. I remember another thing; I remember not really caring a whole lot about being in school. I wanted to be elsewhere doing other things.

And I did just about everything. Break and enter, car theft, a whole variety of activities. It wasn't big, like part of a gang. I think it became that later on. At first it was more individual. But then it was like an education. You become more aware of who the guys are that are getting into trouble, and as your awareness increases, you begin to associate more with them rather than square-job kind of people. I guess that's kind of like a group consciousness sort of thing.

My parents separated when I was young – 1959, I believe – and I ended up staying with my father initially, with my three brothers. But my home life was not all that pleasant, for me anyways, you know, being from a broken home. I was the oldest as well, which meant that there were more responsibilities placed on me to look after my younger brothers, like when I came back from school – preparing meals and taking care of the house, and those kinds of things.

My father was working at the time, and we went through a number of different housekeepers. So, the home life wasn't a whole lot, you know, wasn't easy. Today I would probably have done things differently, knowing that hindsight is 20/20.

I saw my older half-brother, for example, two years ago for the first time in twenty years. I have seen one of my brothers a couple of times. I've seen another brother once. One of them is dead. That one I haven't seen since I've been incarcerated. He passed away – leukemia. My brother Art was the next youngest, and he's working with computers for a firm in Saskatoon right now. My brother Roy, he's involved in construction; and Brian ... I don't know what Brian is doing – that's my older half brother – I don't know what he's doing right now. He works at a lot of different jobs.

Before coming to prison? Well, I drove trucks. Worked as a short-order cook. Worked as a chef in a restaurant, on the night shift, you know, those kinds of jobs. I was into the cooking field. I enjoyed cooking.

I'm thirty-nine in a few days. I was nineteen, with a life bit. My sentence was life, and life at that time was ten-year minimum. But just because you have a minimum doesn't necessarily mean that you're going to get parole. For example, I was eligible for day parole, under the old law, after three years. I still haven't even made day parole. Just four years ago I started going out on UTAs. Unescorted temporary absences. Unescorted temporary absence is with a sponsor, so, in other words I'm not even going out on my own. It's not a true, unescorted temporary absence. It's escorted by citizens who've been willing to do that for me.

Let's see. My hesitation is ... where to begin. It was a typical Friday night for me at that particular time. A group of us that hung around together, we were all at the hotel, and we were looking to continue on with our evening. We ended up at my place later on for a party. That broke up, and then we went to a regular kind of haunt over at my friend's place who lived in the north end. And the irony, this is where the irony really begins to take part, I met my brother that night, for the first time in I don't know how long.

It was one of my younger brothers, my brother Ron, who is a little more than a year younger than me. I hadn't seen him for quite a while. He had been living in Saskatoon but had moved to Winnipeg, and was staying with one of my aunts. And he ended up driving me home that night which was really unusual, as normally on the weekends I would stay at my friend's place.

I had gone through a relationship with a girl that I met in high school, and we had planned to get married and all those kinds of wild, wonderful things, but we had recently broken off, and I was still distressed by that. I recently had gotten out of the pen. I did a two-year sentence for indecent assault, breaking and entering, theft. I think this was the extent of the list. And I was really still wrapped up in her.

My mother had called the party and was wondering what was going on, and we got into this long conversation. I was looking for someplace to blame for the breakup of my relationship. I blamed my mother, blamed a lot of other circumstances.

Anyways I drank a lot that night. My drinking had kind of escalated from not drinking, from when I got out of the pen, to drinking real heavily, and I must have drank at least a case of twenty-four beer myself that night. So, I was really pissed. Plus, I had connections with a number of the truck drivers, and was eating berries [amphetamines] as well, so I was drinking and mixing drugs. That's the kind of mind set that I was in at that particular time.

I ended up breaking into the apartment next door, and the major part of my crime I suppose would be a sexual assault on the woman that was living there. It was kind of like a release. All this kind of sexual frustration and tension, and all the rest of it. I woke up the next morning not even realizing what I had done the night before. As a matter of fact, my cousin came and woke me up the next morning, and we were watching the World Curling Championship when the police arrived and questioned me the first time. It was pretty gruesome. I wish I could turn back the clock. Anyway the police arrested me. I knew about being in the penitentiary system. I had been there, and I knew I was going back; however, I certainly wasn't prepared for the kinds of things that were about to take place.

For about the first week, or ten days or so, after I was charged, I was totally isolated. I had a twenty-four-hour watch on me, and that was for suicide prevention. And I slept a lot, I slept a lot in terms of first of all to get rid of the alcohol, and that kind of thing. I got real sick at that time as well. A little later I got pneumonia and pleurisy, and almost died there. And then there was the long wait. I was arrested in March, my crime took place in March, and I was convicted in October. So there was that long stay, both in the cells in Winnipeg, in the public safety building, the cop shop, and then, after my summary hearing, in remand in Headingly, in the provincial institution. So there was a long period of time in there.

After I was convicted, I didn't know that, see … strange as it may sound, I don't think a lot of people really understand the full crux of what it means to take another life, and to get a life sentence and all the rest. The average citizen doesn't know that, doesn't know a thing about the whole process of the law. I certainly didn't. I was, like I said, I was eighteen when my crime occurred, and when I was nineteen I was doing a life bit. It was really strange, it was really foreign. It was at least a couple of years before it sunk in.

See, for the first sixteen months after my conviction, I was in total isolation. That's what makes it really difficult. I was taken right from the remand centre, and placed right into the hole at Stoney. I spent sixteen months in the hole not communicating with anyone, other than visits from my folks and a psychiatrist calling me up and trying to determine what, if anything, my future was going to be about. I think I finally woke up to what was happening when I turned twenty-one, and the enormity of it struck me.

I think there's a lot of confusion, confusion on the part of the administrative body. There's been a certain amount of rebellion on my part, an unwillingness, for example, to participate in some of the programs – and an arrogance, which I've developed over the years.

See, I've got a heavy psychological contradiction on my file. There are people who see me as being this monster, and I will continue to be this monster, and that's the way I am. And until I go through, for example, until I go through RPC and do their sex offender program, I won't get anything. And yet, there's this other side, including RPC itself, who say, he doesn't need this program. He would not benefit by the program. And so, I've got, I've got this contradiction, and until someone stands up and says, let this guy out and give him a chance, I'm going to stay here. It's something I've been battling with for the last, oh, almost ten years, and it's just been going on and on.

You see, I'm not sure whether I made a mistake or not, but after I came out of the hole, those sixteen months that I spent in the hole in Stoney, I was scheduled to be transferred to this institution right here. And at the last hour before my transfer, I was approached by the psychiatrist and he said, we are opening up this new facility called the Regional Psychiatric Centre, in British Columbia. Would you be willing to go there? My natural curiosity at that time was, yes, I want to go there, I wanted whatever help I could get. I wanted to find out if I was crazy or not. What made me do what I did. You know, what made me participate in crimes that I had participated in. I went there. I spent another sixteen months there.

I went through programs. I went through individual therapy, group therapy, you name it. Whatever was there, I participated in it. Finally, after sixteen months of finding out and realizing that I wasn't crazy, wasn't psycho or psychopathic or whatever, I began to find myself. I began to realize all of a sudden, okay, I've learned all these things, now I have to apply those things into my life. And that's when the battles started.

The first person I ran up against was Bob Cross who was head of transfers at that time, and he says, no, we will not transfer you to Mountain. We will transfer you back to Stoney Mountain. That was their policy and I didn't like that very much because it was sort of like throwing me back into the fire, because I knew that there was absolutely nothing in Stoney Mountain for me, other than going back to the hole and spending a lot of isolated time again. Which is exactly what happened. I spent a further nine months in the hole, in protective custody. It was a bitter, bitter time for me in that respect.

I finally got here in February 1975. For the first time I began to feel a sense of freedom, being able to feel alive anyways, feel that I could play some games, or put my life together. I think leaving Stoney Mountain, leaving the prairies, was in one sense running away from my crime and that part of my life, and having the opportunity to kind of, like, start all over. And NELOF ended up being one of those areas where I was able to find a lot more of myself, become involved with the Native side of myself. I had to learn what it meant to be a Native, what it meant to identify with that particular cultural group rather than what my past case history was about. I had to, kind of like, almost disregard that, and learn something new. So I had to learn, and that was why I became involved in not only NELOF, but Native spirituality, working with the Native Brotherhood club, finding out what a potlatch was for the first time, and pow-wows, and what the elders were about, and all those kinds of things. That, to me, was a restructuring, things that I didn't have before, and I had to set in place inside myself, before I could identify with, you know, the impact of my offence, my crime. At some point you have to, as a lifer, you have to turn that around. You've got to hit the bottom. When I was in the hole in Stoney, that was my journey to hell, that was my journey into the pit. Somehow, I had to go from there to the top, or, scratch my way to the top. Another piece of that for me has been the education department. Being associated with them for the last eight years did not help much either. I'm beginning to realize that education per se is not what we make it out to be.

The promises that the government and the mission statement make have not filtered down to guys like me – and lifers in general. It's not intended for us. It's intended for those guys who are coming into the system for a short period of time, that they'll be treated well, and that they'll be respected. But for guys who are doing long-term sentences, we're at the mercy of the powers that be. We have, I have, no recourse to say to them, You're wrong, you made a mistake, you made an error. Once they make a recommendation and it goes down in black and white, then I have to live with that and deal with that for the rest of my life.

Something that they should do but wouldn't do, for example, is create an institution or facility for us lifers, and lump us together. I think it would provide a stronger support system while we're doing the time, and I think it would also force the administration to deal with – to deal with all of us, rather than dealing with us, as they are, on this really individualistic basis, keeping us separated so we as lifers have virtually no recourse, like no recourse to address our documentation, for example.

I've met a lot of lifers over the years, and most of them are, once you get over the initial hurdle of being separated from your family, and I've lost virtually all contact with my family other than just the superficial kind of relationship, the lifers become your comrades. They become the guys you really become close to. Like my association with Glen, and Ivan, and a couple of other guys down in the compound, those are the guys that I really feel close to. I've got twenty years in, so I don't really feel that close to the short-timers that are coming in, because they're just like shadows, I suppose.

It's like lifers, they pick out their own kind of corner, or find out their own little niches inside the institution. Most lifers are respected in many ways, just because of the amount of time they've had in, or the fact that they're doing a life sentence, or whatever. There's a certain amount of respect.

So, if you had an institution where it was all just lifers, I think you'd get a real powerful situation where people could make changes in their life. We could genuinely get a lot more success in terms of doing things. First of all, what would happen is, like, lifers would become involved in something, would become involved with some kind of productivity. Most lifers that I know of really feel empathy about their past life, what they've done. And they struggle and they do things to try and make up for that. They keep trying a number of different things, projects, or involvement in groups or clubs, or whatever, and they keep putting themselves out.

And if you had a place like that, the administration would also have to supply the expertise in order to deal with that. In other words, we would automatically have to have the professional people – the psychologists and psychiatrists and whatever, that would be necessary. If there was an institution that had a lot of lifers, then the administration would be forced to deal with us, and forced to deal with us not only as individuals, but as a group, because all of a sudden we have all these individuals who are high-priority, high-focus, and some high-risk. But see, I think the biggest mistake is that they have most of us classified as high-risk in terms of dangerousness, when a lot of lifers aren't dangerous whatsoever. They're some of the most passive people I've ever met. But because of certain conditions, whether it's drugs, or alcohol, or whatever else, those kinds of crimes are moments of spontaneity in their life. But for the rest of the time, they're not a problem, they're not a threat. They're certainly not a threat to me. Of all my time in prison, I have never been threatened by a lifer. But I have been by others, certainly.

You know, a friend of mine, another lifer, said it. He said that the system doesn't even realize what they have. What will keep him out, as well as me probably, is the fact that you've got a lot of your short-timers and a lot of people who are real pricks, real assholes, or real deviants, or, or really sick bastards. And it's those guys that'll keep me out – because I know what they're like and I wouldn't want to associate with them. And the system doesn't even realize that they have that. For the most part I ignore them, but if it comes to aggression, or being aggressive, in terms of protection or whatever, I could be as assertive as anyone else.

Surprisingly, a lot of short-timers come to me for advice. In terms of addressing, for example, a psychological assessment, or what do you recommend, or do you think I should go to RPC? For the most part it doesn't bother me. It bothers me some and I wish I was in their place, you know, I wish I was getting out, I wish it was my turn. But my turn's going to come soon. Living the illusion, living the dream, eh.

When I get out? Oh, for the first little while I think it's play. I want to go out and play, I want to go out and have fun. When I say play, I mean get away from the tension and the monotonous, boring, day-after-day kind of routines. I want to go out and have fun and enjoy myself, and be with people, be with friends. I mean, because in here, a lot of the times, you're not. With all the people around here, I'm not being with a lot of them, right?

As far as a job, well, economics and material things are probably the farthest things from my mind. And that's not only from being in prison and having to do without for so long, it's that that aspect of life would probably be one of the things I'd really have to learn about. Learn over again, learn how to pay the rent, and food, and learn, kind of like the basic necessities of life.

UPDATE

Lance had been out on day parole for a couple of months in the fall of 1992, but it had been revoked when, while registered in courses at SFU to meet the qualifying work for his admission into a master's program, a serious misunderstanding with one of the support staff resulted in a letter to his parole officer about his "threatening behaviour." He was now back at Mountain Institution, but had a parole hearing coming up shortly and hoped to be admitted to a work camp up north, designed specifically for long-term offenders and their preparation for gradual release into the community.

He thought that he "couldn't have done anything differently to change the impression of me" when out on day parole. He hadn't realized how fast the pace could be out there. He had never thought of coming back, "that was the furthest thing from my mind." But "guys in prison have not an iota of sense about what it means to work eight to twelve hours a day, to hold down a regular job in outside time." Since he'd come back in, he'd put a "turtle shell" around himself: he felt that he'd "let everyone down" and felt "guilt, some anger, though not as much as hurt, frustration." He had put in twenty-one years before his day parole and just wondered when it would all end: he lived his crimes everyday, he would "never escape that, but when would enough be enough?"; he had "forgotten the details" – it was "like a video without sound." He admitted that his goals, when he'd been out, had been perhaps "too broad and generalized" – "prison does that to you, you have to think generalities, not specifics." It's hard "to live a dream" and he sees himself as a "visionary person."

Lance's parole application was successful in the fall of 1995.

EPILOGUE

Those sentenced to life-25 were indeed one of the most neglected groups in the prison population during the period following the abolition of capital punishment in 1976. After sentencing by the courts these lifers were warehoused by the Correctional Service of Canada, replete with a written account of the particulars of the "merchandise," prices and charges annexed. Then silence – broken by the outcry a decade or so later over the judicial review at fifteen years.

The immediate rhetorical contexts of our project, who is speaking to whom for what purpose, were relatively straightforward: these men were telling us their stories in order to shed some light on the very nature and function of the life-25 sentence. Now that our roles as envoys have made public those views the rhetorical aspects of their telling are, of course, much more complex and indeterminate, dependent upon each reader's reaction. Some of the men interviewed will be regarded as being more convincing and persuasive in the expression of their views than others; some will come across more sympathetically than others … But one feature which will strike any reader is that many of the men we interviewed did not really have much of a life of their own before they ended up doing life-25. A whole complex web of social problems lies behind their actions and needs to be ciphered into the questions concerning "premeditation" – dysfunctional families, child abuse, mental illness, diminished capacity due to drug and alcohol problems, questions of race and class – to name only the most obvious instances. These issues aside, however, and keeping our focus on the life-25 sentences themselves, what sense can be made of such very long periods of incarceration, what rationale besides that of punishment pure and simple can be put forth? The inescapable fact is that these sentences do not make sense – except that they were an unsatisfactory political compromise reached in the midst of the heated debate over capital punishment.

More reasonable and just alternatives to life-25 would involve doing away with the distinction between first and second-degree murder and then lowering the period of parole eligibility to ten years (serial murderers, the Olsons and Bernardos, would be excluded from such proposed reforms; they would serve mandatory life sentences without parole). Yet such progressive reforms, which have been advanced by criminologists such as Neil Boyd and Thomas O'Reilly-Fleming, are routinely excluded from even being seriously considered in the midst of the public furor, media "debate," and political manoeuvring which have enveloped the judicial review at fifteen years. Hence any thoughtful consideration of what the life-25 sentence actually entails is stonewalled as the political agenda is pushed further and further to the right, with the ironic – yet predictable – consequence that Justice Minister Allan Rock's recent amendments to the judicial review process, in that they did not totally scrap the existing provisions, appeared as somehow "liberal" in nature, when they were clearly anything but that. (See "Appendix: Section 745 of the Criminal Code and Recent Amendments," on page 205, for more details.) Given the present political climate in this regard, and no significant changes are foreseeable, it would therefore be totally unrealistic to expect any serious re-thinking of the life-25 sentence in terms of more enlightened and effective policies and directives.

What is left then? If the life-25 sentences are to remain as fixtures of the Canadian criminal justice system, we should at least demand that they serve some constructive purposes (this is a veritable refrain of the men we interviewed, however diverse their backgrounds). Appropriate and effective programming needs to be developed for those serving life-25. The Commissioner's Task Force on Long-Term Sentences, whose thirty-seven recommendations were approved for implementation in 1991, was designed to address this very situation; but it is clear from the interviews, particularly the updates, that comprehensive and effective programming is not yet fully operational. The *Report of the Task Force* endorsed a management and intervention model based on the Palmer principle, which maintains that all sentences should be broken down into four measurable segments: adaptation (accepting the sentence); integration into the prison environment (institutionalization, in the more affirmative sense of taking full advantage of opportunities for personal growth inside prison); preparation for release (de-institutionalization, with a focus on the release process); and, finally, return to society (helping inmates adapt to outside life). These changes in management policies undeniably were an improvement over the situation we encountered in the interviews with men who had served a significant number of years (five or more) prior to 1991 and these new strategies. Many of these men had had virtually no contact with prison personnel in terms of developing a correctional plan; indeed, many told us they were left to work out their own plans for doing their time and this meant for most of them at least a five-year stay at Kent Maximum Security, hardly the most congenial of places for rehabilitative programs. Since 1991, the policy has been to move the life-25 group more quickly to lower security institutions ("cascading" is the CSC term for this), in order to break up an essentially time-wasting regime that lacks any substantial programming directives. This more flexible transfer policy obviously has benefitted some of the men we interviewed.

The most dramatic programming intervention encountered by the men we interviewed was the eight-month personality disorder program (dealing with both sex offenders and violent offenders), offered at the Regional Health Centre in Matsqui. Here, in a therapeutic community setting, the emphasis was placed on interlocking modules that fostered "self-help" skills and the need to assume responsibility, leading to the prevention of continued dysfunctional/deviant behaviors. Requirements for admission to the program are voluntary admission of guilt to a sexual offense or violent offense and a primary motivation to change. With a few reservations, these programs were regarded very positively by the men we interviewed. The problem is, of course, that for men looking at twenty-five-year minimum sentences, this eight-month segment, however valuable it might be, is swallowed up by the enormous length of time still to be served. And this time will have to be done in their "home" institutions where the therapeutic/rehabilitative programming they have received comes into conflict with the prison sub-culture with its "con code," the "two solitudes" of the protective custody/general population split, the various other cliques which form around the drug trade etc., double-bunking and overcrowding – all of which militate against the delivery of successful programming. Life in this most artificially contrived of societies can, as many of the interviews testify, revert to a state of nature in which existence can be nasty, brutish and long.

The RHC programs need to be completed as part of the applicant's judicial review program if he is to have any hope of success. So the question becomes: when is the optimum time to go through it? The life-25 prisoner's own needs are often in conflict with the planning required for a successful judicial review. CSC programming is still very much a case of "stop and go" and "hurry up and wait." The basic problem remains that these sentences are – in human terms – much too long to organize in a constructive fashion. For a person serving life-25, the Inmate Correctional Treatment

Program includes modules such as "cognitive living skills," "breaking barriers," and other short courses which can be neatly ticked off in the appropriate boxes. But how many times can one profitably take these life skills courses when any possibility of testing them out seems light years away? Just how serious the CSC is about developing and implementing long-range planning for lifers is further cast in doubt by the fact that only two years after the Task Force completed its report all university programs in federal prisons were terminated. The Simon Fraser University Prison Education Program in the Pacific Region was internationally renowned and served as the model for similar programs in the United States and Great Britain. It had demonstrably proven its worth over a twenty-year period and effectively combined academic and living skills for personal growth. Moreover, its credibility as an outside agency would seem to foster those very connections with the community and society at large which are such a key component of the final stage of the four-part CSC management model. In short, there is a long way to go before the objectives of the 1989 mission statement of the CSC in terms of programming can be met: "We must acknowledge that a minority of offenders will not be returning to the community for many years to come, and that some offenders may never be released. However, all offenders must have opportunities to serve their sentences in a meaningful and dignified manner and our programs must provide for personal growth within the institutional setting."

The testimony of the men we interviewed shows that these aims are still largely rhetorical in nature and have yet to be translated into the realities of prison life. It is hardly surprising, then, that many prisoners have ironically dubbed the guiding principles of the CSC as "Mission Impossible." For many prisoners, and especially for those serving life-25, prison time is still often "down time" in which they are simply warehoused.

We are all, however, affected by this process: the cost of housing prisoners varies from approximately $30,000 a year in minimum security prisons to about three times that much in maximum-security prisons. The new amendments to Section 745 will mean that hundreds of prisoners who would be legitimate candidates for parole will remain housed at taxpayer expense, with no hope of release, whereas study after study has clearly shown that paroled murderers seldom commit other crimes. This is, of course, only the most obvious and literal type of warehousing, however important the fiscal considerations might be in today's political context. With reference to the most serious of all crimes, first-degree murder, our practical, ethical, and imaginative judgments are pushed to the uttermost limits. Above all, we need to tax our imaginations in the search for constructive and acceptable alternatives to the life-25 sentence.

APPENDIX

Section 745 of the Criminal Code and Recent Amendments

Under Section 745 of the Criminal Code, prisoners sentenced to life are not eligible for parole until they have served twenty-five years of their sentence, *unless* they are successful in their fifteen-year judicial review, which can bring forward the date of parole eligibility. As the first candidates for judicial review came forward in the late 1980s, Section 745 was often referred to as a "little-known" amendment to the Criminal Code that had been languishing on the books since 1976. Since then it has indeed become widely known, and has often been labeled the "faint-hope" clause. It has often been mockingly termed an "escape" clause, a "loophole", a "time-out" that somehow suspends the proper functioning of the judicial process, and a "forty percent sentence discount" (by the Canadian Police Association). Here is how Section 745 read *before* amendments enacted in the Fall 1996 session of Parliament:

(1) Where a person has served at least fifteen years of his sentence
    (a) in the case of a person who has been convicted of high treason or first-degree murder,
    (b) in the case of a person convicted of second-degree murder who has been sentenced to imprisonment for life without eligi-

bility for parole until he has served more than fifteen years of his sentence, he may apply to the appropriate Chief Justice in the province in which the conviction took place for a reduction in his number of years of imprisonment without eligibility for parole.

(2) Upon receipt of an application under subsection (1), the appropriate Chief Justice shall designate a judge of the superior court of criminal jurisdiction to empanel a jury to hear the application and determine whether the applicant's number of years of imprisonment without eligibility for parole ought to be reduced having regard to the character of the applicant, his conduct while serving his sentence, the nature of the offense for which he was convicted and such other matters as the judge deems relevant in the circumstances and the determination shall be made by no less than two-thirds of the jury.

(3) Where the jury hearing an application under subsection (1) determines that the applicant's number of years of imprisonment without eligibility for parole ought not to be reduced, the jury shall set another time at or after which an application may again be made by the applicant to the appropriate Chief Justice for a reduction in his number of years of imprisonment without eligibility for parole.

(4) Where the jury hearing an application under subsection (1) determines that the applicant's number of years of imprisonment without eligibility for parole ought to be reduced, the jury may, by order:

(a) substitute a lesser number of years of imprisonment without eligibility for parole than that then applicable; or

(b) terminate the ineligibility for parole.

(5) The appropriate Chief Justice in each province or territory may make such rules in respect of applications and hearings under this section as are required for the purposes of this section.

On March 12, 1996, NDP MP Nelson Riis re-introduced Liberal MP John Nunziata's Private Member's Bill calling for the elimination of Section 745. Riis is representative of the many politicians who have raised their voices in calling for the elimination of Section 745 in his emphasis upon victims' rights over those of prisoners, as if the two were mutually exclusive: "There's a rising tide of rage as people find out about this section. The victims are going to be put through all their misery again." And, as in virtually every discussion of Section 745, the high-profile cases of serial murderers Clifford Olson and Paul Bernardo are identified with the possibility of the convicted somehow duping the system and obtaining release before a full sentence has been completed. This is highly misleading since life-25 should always be read as a minimum sentence; that is, it is really an indeterminate sentence. Hence it is obvious that the Olsons and Bernardos would never set foot outside of prison given the present legislation. Nevertheless, it would appear that Section 745 will be amended to take into account cases such as Olson (who was technically eligible for application for judicial review in the summer of 1996): those serving concurrent life-25 sentences would henceforth be excluded from eligibility to seek judicial review. Justice Minister Allan Rock has been talking about making such revision, but has resisted demands to repeal completely Section 745. Rock has gone on record as stating there are "exceptional cases" where early release is justified and has added that any changes to early parole rules for murderers will reflect concerns of victims' families, but will also take into account the humane treatment of killers. National Parole Board Chair Willie Gibbs also affirmed early in 1996 that he does not support any Private Member's Bill that would sweep away Section 745: "I think it gives an opportunity for review at about the right time."

On June 11, 1996, Rock introduced legislation to amend Section 745 that would prevent murderers guilty of multiple killings from being eligible to apply, and all other applications would be vetted by a judge to screen out ones unlikely to succeed. Another proposed amendment would require all twelve members of a jury to support any decision to reduce the parole eligibility date (at present only a two-thirds majority is required). Members of the Bloc Québecois refused to give consent to the proposed amendments, thereby preventing the bill from getting a third reading and passing before the end of the summer session of Parliament. Bloc Québecois house leader Gilles Duceppe stated: "We opposed the bill because after fifteen years, maybe it's possible to rehabilitate the inmate." Justice Minister Rock made it clear, however, that the government was committed to enacting these amendments; it was simply a question of time: "Even if this legislation is not enacted until later this year, the overall purpose is to improve the criminal justice system."

These amendments were eventually passed in the Fall 1996 session of Parliament. Whether they have in fact improved the criminal justice system is, however, highly debatable. Newly released cabinet documents show that in 1976 then Prime Minister Pierre Trudeau insisted, in the face of opposition within his cabinet and the Liberal caucus, that the so-called faint-hope clause that allowed for judical review at fifteen years must be maintained in the legislation that did away with capital punishment. "The prime minister objected strongly to the removal of this provision, asserting that the proposed legislation was already 'Neanderthal' enough without adding to its repressive character," the cabinet minutes report. "In his view, between maintaining capital punishment and sending people to jail for twenty-five years with no hope of being released, the former might well be considered less cruel."

Now, twenty years later, these provisions have in principle been fundamentally altered. Many potential applicants for judicial review and their laywers now regard the faint-hope clause as being in practice the "ain't-a-hope clause". Recently released 1997 statistics from the CSC reveal, that even before these new amendments were enacted, only a third of those convicted of first-degree murder exercised their eligibility to apply for judicial review and that within this group there is, contrary to public opinion, a dramatic absence of any significant pattern of success in gaining substantial reductions of the life-25 sentence.

BIBLIOGRAPHY

Annotated entries focus on issues which are particularly relevant to the life-25 sentence: the academic debate over the effects of such long-term sentences on those who must serve them, and the public debate over what the life-25 sentence should mean and how it should be administered.

Bennett, James, 1981. *Oral History and Delinquency: The Rhetoric of Criminology.* Chicago and London: University of Chicago Press.

Bennett raises a host of intriguing historical as well as philosophical questions about the role of oral narratives within the discipline of criminology. The follow-ing comment is, for example, particularly interesting in terms of our objective in Life-25 to let the interviewees try to describe their experiences of imprisonment: "The oral history is wrong even to attempt to convey the essential horror of incarceration because the inevitable failure is concealed: the reader is deceived into thinking he has been 'on the inside', whereas a candid and humble admis-sion of the collapse of language before such extraordinary reality would be the only means of even beginning to gain imaginative entrance."

Boyd, Neil, 1988. *The Last Dance: Murder in Canada.* Prentice-Hall Canada (Seal edition, 1992).

Boyd attempts "to combine academic analysis with popular culture," drawing together an historical-critical survey and excerpts from interviews with thirty-five men and five women who have been convicted of first or second-degree mur-der. In his "Introduction," Boyd states: "The twenty-five-year mandatory minimum term for first degree murder could be lowered to ten years in peniten-tiary and the current ten-year mandatory term for second-degree murder could be lowered to five years in penitentiary - without any identifiable loss in com-

munity safety."

Claridge, Thomas, 1992. "Crime and Punishment" ["Killers who are calling time out"], *Toronto Globe and Mail*, July 4, pp. D1, D4.

This article is interesting for it appeared at a time when the issue of the fifteen-year judicial review was beginning to figure prominently in public debates. The sub-heading suggests that "killers" are somehow calling an illegal "time out" and that the game is not being played fairly.

_____, 1997. "Only third of killers eligible seek parole review." *Toronto Globe and Mail*, January 4, p. A6.

This is a very useful breakdown of CSC statistics on the number of applicants for judicial review and the general lack of success experienced by those who have gone through the process. Also of particular interest is the fact that in Ontario "most of those who hypothetically could benefit from the controversial Code provision have not even bothered to apply for reviews," whereas in Quebec most of the applications succeed and "the reductions obtained from Quebec juries have been greater qualitatively as well as quantitatively."

Cohen, Stanley and Laurie Taylor, 1972. (1981, second edition with a postscript by John McVicar). *Psychological Survival: The Experience of Long-Term Imprisonment.* London: Penguin.

A "collaborative research project" undertaken with the prisoners of E-Wing, Durham Prison. Chapter 4, "Time and Deterioration," deals with the prisoners' fears of turning into passive consumers of "prison time."

Coker, J. and J. P. Martin, 1985. *Licensed to Live.* Oxford: Basil Blackwell.

The authors marshall evidence which indicates that the effects of long-term incarceration might be largely reversible. Little work has been done in this area and much more is clearly required.

Duguid, Stephen, 1993. *"Cognitive Dissidents Bite the Dust — The Demise of University Education in Canada's Prisons." Convergence,* Vol. XXVI, No. 3, pp. 51-59.

Penetrating analysis of the reasons behind the cancellation of university programs, pointing out that "the convenient excuse of fiscal shortages" masks "the new correctional system" which was focused on the "criminogenic factors that led to crime and imprisonment."

Ekstedt, John W. and Curt T. Griffiths, 1988 (second edition). *Corrections in Canada: Policy and Practice*. Toronto and Vancouver: Butterworths.

This is an excellent introduction for anyone seeking an overview of the history and development of the Corrections system in Canada. In the section on "The Capital Punishment Debate," they point out that, "with the death penalty unavailable, the psychology of decision making tends to press for the use of the life sentence in a disproportionate way, so that there is an increase in the numbers of persons serving life sentences."

Haley, Hugh J., 1984. "Does the Law Need to Know the Effects of Imprisonment?" *Canadian Journal of Criminology*, Vol. 26, No. 4, pp. 479-491.

Haley draws attention to the fact that the punitiveness of a sentence is measured by its duration and not by its effects; hence there is a lack of clear policy directives in terms of what is to be done with offenders within the prison. This problem is particularly acute for those with an indeterminate sentence such as life-25.

Hall, Neal, 1995. "System on Parole," *Vancouver Sun*, February 4, A1, A3 (first in a four part series).

Media discussion of the parole issue, particularly with reference to the fifteen-year judicial review for those convicted of first-degree murder, has often been little more than tabloid sensationalism. This series is a case in point: while Hall's article begins by making some serious points about the statistical reality of parole which is out of sync with "public perception," his views are lost sight of (literally) in the very layout of the front pages of the Vancouver Sun – the words "public perception" on the left-hand side of the page flow directly to the photo of a woman's arm reaching out to touch a picture of Melanie Carpenter at the memorial service for this young woman who was abducted and murdered. The right-hand column deals with this memorial service and it is as if the would-be discussion of the serious issues at stake has been completely side-tracked.

McKay, H. Bryan, *et al.*, 1979. *The Effects of Long-Term Incarceration and a Proposed Strategy for Future Research*. Ottawa: Ministry of the Solicitor General.

Commenting on the lack of knowledge about the effects of long-term incarceration, McKay describes the area as a "methodological nightmare" which is not easily accommodated by approaches employing systematic empirical verification: "One of the strongest impressions to emerge in reviewing long-term con-

finement literature is the striking discrepancy between personal accounts and the data-based research describing it."

Marron, Kevin, 1996. *Slammer: The Crisis in Canada's Prison System.* Toronto: Doubleday Canada.

A journalistic tour of Canada's federal prisons, highlighting key problem areas such as overcrowding; points out the gap between theoretical intentions and the actual ability to deliver on program initiatives.

Mitchell, Barry, 1990. *Murder and Penal Policy.* New York: St. Martin's.

In this study of long-term imprisonment policies in England and Wales, Mitchell agrees with Roger Sapsford that there is no conclusive evidence of deterioration as a result of lengthy imprisonment, but adds that prisoners need to be involved in group work so as to break down social barriers and be encouraged to develop outside-world contacts. They also require someone to listen to and understand them: "No specific person could be identified to fulfil this role, but whoever it is should encourage open communication, permit the prisoner to discuss his problems and simply let him talk."

Morrison, Campbell, 1996. "Trudeau backed faint hope clause." *Vancouver Sun*, November 12, pp. A1-A2.

Information now available under the Access to Information Act shows that in a cabinet meeting on February 6, 1976, Prime Minister Pierre Trudeau insisted that the judicial review at fifteen years be kept as a key component of the legislative package that abolished capital punishment later that year. Trudeau also strongly rejected another caucus proposal that would have retained capital punishment for those convicted of a second murder, arguing that "capital punishment was either to be abolished or not."

O'Reilly-Fleming, Thomas, 1992. "'The Dark Workshop': Life Sentences, Prison Conditions and the Politics of Punishment." Chapter 12 in *Canadian Penology: Advanced Perspectives*, ed. Kevin McCormick and Livy Visano, pp. 291-321. Toronto: Canadian Scholars Press.

Strongly and passionately argued critique of the whole policy of life sentences. O'Reilly-Fleming's argument for "scrapping the fifteen-year review" and replacing it with a number of "reasonable alternatives" is especially interesting within the contexts of the life-25 controversy.

Palmer, William R. T., 1983. *The Effects of Long-Term Incarceration: Programs for Long-Term Offenders.* Ottawa: Correctional Service of Canada.

Report presented at the Second World Congress on Prison Health Care, held in Ottawa in August 1983. This is an important paper, as its proposed four-stage management model was adopted in the Report of the Task Force on Long-Term Sentences *in 1991: adaptation, integration, preparation for release, and return to society.*

_____ 1984. "Programming for Long-Term Inmates: A New Perspective," in *The Canadian Journal of Criminology*, Vol. 26, No. 4, pp. 439-457.

This is a report on the LifeServers program operating in Warkworth Institution since 1976. A description of the program is given as well as discussion and recommendation for providing "discrete units" for the housing of long-term offenders.

Parker, Tony, 1990. *Life After Life: Interviews with Twelve Murderers.* London: Secker and Warburg.

Parker is a master of the taped interview and his work on prison related areas has, above all, brought out the humanistic issues which are so often lost sight of in the imposition of various social science research grids. In his preface, Parker makes a point that is certainly also valid in the Canadian context: "'For life' means for life. A lifer may however at some stage be allowed out of prison on license, to continue serving the sentence in the community under the supervision of a probation officer, on strict conditions."

_____ 1995. *The Violence of Our Lives: Interviews with Life-Sentence Prisoners in America.* London: HarperCollins.

A similar book to Life After Life, with people in the U.S. who are in the same position, either in prison for murder or on the outside on probation after having served their sentence for murder. Concluding section switches perspective and gives the views of the "victims."

Porporino, Frank, ed. *Forum on Corrections Research*, Vol. 4, No. 2, June 1992.

"This issue of Forum summarizes the findings of the Task Force on Long-Term Sentences (1991) and includes a major review of the literature on the effects of incarceration by Dr. Timothy Flanagan, one of the most notable academic

experts in the area." This is a very useful reference guide, supplying an overview of the problems attendant on the life-25 sentence; but it should be kept in mind that Forum is published for "the staff and management of the Correctional Service of Canada."

Riis, Nelson, Spring 1996. *Riis Report* ("Help Repeal Section 745," p. 5).

A cut-out petition form is prefaced as follows: "I have co-sponsored a Private Member's Bill, C-226, in Parliament which would repeal Section 745 of the Criminal Code of Canada. This clause in the Criminal Code guarantees all convicted first-degree murderers serving life sentences an opportunity to reduce their parole ineligibility after serving only fifteen years. Section 745 has created an imbalance in our justice system. If you wish to support the repeal of Section 745, fill out the petition below and mail it back to me."

Sapsford, Roger, 1983. *Life Sentence Prisoners: Reaction, Response and Change.* Milton Keynes: Open University Press.

Sapsford argues that Cohen and Taylor in Psychological Survival do not demonstrate that deterioration actually does occur as a result of long-term imprisonment; on the contrary, prisoners survive by means of the "amazing" human ability to find ways of coping. The weighting of his last sentence should, however, be carefully considered: "This says nothing for the conditions of the men's imprisonment or for the society which finds it 'necessary' to impose such conditions, but much for the 'nature' of human nature."

Serge, Victor, 1977. *Men in Prison.* London: Writers and Readers Publishing Cooperative.

The novel, first published in 1931, documents Serge's experiences as a political prisoner in French jails from 1912 to 1917. It is one of the most powerful and insightful works to deal with the prison experience, and his comments on the irreparable change which imprisonment effects – "I was no longer a man, but a man in prison" (from the opening chapter, "Arrest") – should be carefully compared with contemporary social science research that argues for the ameliorative aspects of incarceration.

Silverman, Robert and Leslie Kennedy, 1993. *Deadly Deeds: Murder in Canada.* Scarborough: Nelson Canada.

A comprehensive review of the explanations of murder, "drawing upon a detailed data base that presents all occurrences of murder in Canada over the last thirty years." In their "Summing Up", the authors question whether the life-

25 *nonparolable sentence is "reasonable or justifiable on any theoretical grounds. Certainly, it is a longer sentence than that given for first-degree murder in much of the rest of the world where capital punishment has been abolished."*

Toch, Hans and Kenneth Adams, with J. Douglas Grant, 1989. *Coping: Maladaptation in Prisons.* New Brunswick, NJ: Transaction.

One of their "firm conclusions" relates to the maturation potential of maladaptive behaviour: "The longer the imprisonment, the greater the improvement (except for seriously disturbed inmates and 'chronics'), but the greater, also, the inmate's age. This does not mean that age accounts for change, but neither does prison exposure. The older the inmate, and the longer the exposure, the greater the improvement." They conclude that "personal reform [...] can thus prevent much harm to the community over long stretches of time."

Walford, Bonnie, 1987. *Lifers: The Stories of Eleven Women Serving Life Sentences for Murder.* Montreal: Eden Press.

Walford's goal as an "insider" is "to publicize the plight of lifers and to convince the public that literally anyone could find herself in P4W [Prison for Women in Kingston] on a murder conviction. Indeed, most of the lifers here are indistinguishable from the woman next door."

Walker, Nigel, 1987. "The unwanted effects of long-term imprisonment," in A. E. Bottoms and R. Light (eds.), *Problems of Long-Term Imprisonment.* Aldershot: Gower, pp. 183-199.

Argues that research in British prisons has done much "to deflate the sweeping exaggerations [...] about the ill-effects of normal incarceration," but adds "every exaggeration has, by definition, a small hard core of truth, which can be overlooked in the process of deflation. There are live babies in the bathwater."

Wormith, J. S., 1984. "The Controversy Over the Effects of Long-Term Incarceration," in *The Canadian Journal of Criminology*, Vol. 26, No. 4, pp. 423-437.

This is a useful summary of various positions which have been staked out in the debate over long-term imprisonment. Wormith does underline the complex nature of the problem and warns against simplistic solutions; instead, he concludes, we need to ask "the truly important questions," such as, what are the adverse aspects of incarceration, who will experience them, why will they experience them, and how can we ameliorate them?

_____ 1985. "Long-Term Incarceration: Data and Reason Meet Ideology and Rhetoric," in *The Canadian Journal of Criminology*, Vol. 27, pp. 349-357.

Wormith attempts to defend himself and other contributors to a special issue on long-term incarceration (Canadian Journal of Criminology, Vol. 26, No. 4, 1984) against charges that they were defending the status quo in their arguments for the positive effects of such long-term sentences. The article is of value – even if Wormith's defense is not very convincing – since it dramatizes a major schism within the academic community over the whole vexed issue of long-term sentencing.

Zamble, Edward and Frank Porporino, 1988. *Coping, Behaviour, and Adaptation in Prison Inmates.* New York: Springer-Verlag.

From their sample of short term offenders across an average of eighteen months of imprisonment, the authors argue that, contrary to public opinion, there was no significant "deterioration." In a later paper, Zamble extended the time period of his sample across an average of seven years (Coping, Behaviour and Adaptation in Long-Term Prison Inmates, 1992). It is maintained that the inmates' behavioural states generally improved over time. Only three life-25 prisoners were included in this survey; it is, therefore, unclear whether men serving such long sentences would indeed escape "damage."

Zubrycki, R. M., 1984. "Long-term Incarceration in Canada," in *The Canadian Journal of Criminology*, Vol. 26, No. 4, pp. 397-402.

Concluding remarks highlight the lack of knowledge about the effects of long-term incarceration and emphasize that the consequences of the build-up of life-25 prisoners for both the system and the individual are unclear; "therefore, careful study and monitoring of the effects of long-term incarceration is a necessity of future planning."